DECORATIVE BRUSH-WORK
& ELEMENTARY DESIGN

Plate I.

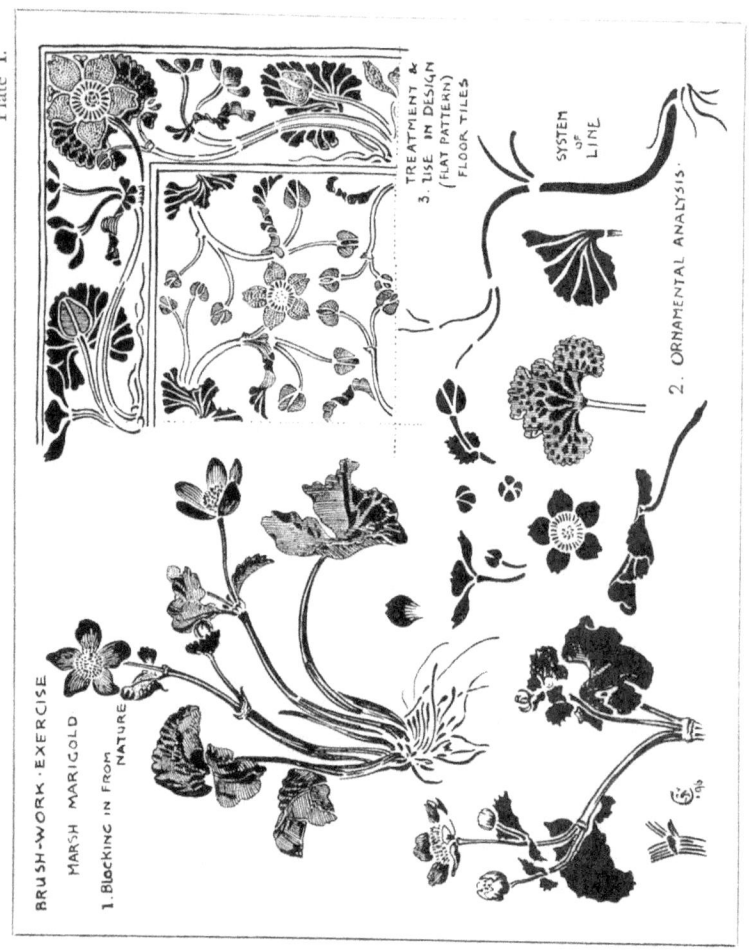

BRUSH-WORK · EXERCISE

MARSH MARIGOLD

1. Blocking in from Nature

2. ORNAMENTAL ANALYSIS.

SYSTEM OF LINE

TREATMENT & 3. USE IN DESIGN (FLAT PATTERN) FLOOR TILES

DECORATIVE BRUSH-WORK
& ELEMENTARY DESIGN

A MANUAL FOR THE USE OF TEACHERS AND STUDENTS IN ELEMENTARY, SECONDARY, AND TECHNICAL SCHOOLS

BY

HENRY CADNESS

SECOND MASTER OF THE MUNICIPAL SCHOOL OF ART, AND
LECTURER IN TEXTILE DESIGN AT THE MUNICIPAL SCHOOL
OF TECHNOLOGY, MANCHESTER.

SECOND EDITION. REVISED AND ENLARGED

WITH FORTY-TWO PLATES, COMPRISING ABOUT FOUR
HUNDRED AND FIFTY EXAMPLES OF DESIGN

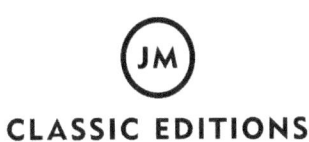

CLASSIC EDITIONS

PREFACE

TO THE SECOND EDITION.

THE issue of a second edition gives an opportunity to thank those who have so generously expressed their appreciation of my work. The press criticisms have been remarkably favourable and encouraging.

It might be urged that certain sections are too advanced to be of use to juniors. Such has happily proved not to be the case. It is possible to set too low an estimate in this subject on elementary teachers and pupils which is not justified by fact, and although there is still a call for ready-made lessons, the teacher soon discovers that such cannot produce the best results. True success can only arise from the personality and taste of the teacher, and therefore, whilst further suggestions are offered in the additional plates, they are chiefly to indicate method and application, it still being left to the teacher to infuse original ideas into the work to suit the class requirements, at the same time, the junior craftsman may find these examples useful as bases to develop for special purposes.

HENRY CADNESS.

DIDSBURY, MANCHESTER,
March, 1904.

PREFACE

My aim in this book is to place before the student a description of the elementary stages of Practical Designing. It is based somewhat on the lines of a course of practice and lectures given by me at the Manchester Municipal Schools of Art and Technology, and consists of seven chapters, comprising twenty-five sections. Of these sections 1 to 5 deal with materials used in designing and useful for brushwork ; 6 and 7, with preparatory work in designing ; 8, with methods of treatment ; 9 to 11, the elementary forms used in ornament ; 12 to 16, Nature studies with brush and colour ; 17 to 22, influences in forming styles ; 23 to 25, the application of study.

The points dwelt upon should become the common

knowledge of all those engaged in the study of Art as applied to the industries, since the methods described for the production of working drawings and for the development of inventive power are applicable to most crafts. To teachers in elementary schools the instructions and examples should prove useful, particularly for the preparation of diagrams and object-lessons.

The suggestions for Nature study may form a fair basis for a loving pursuit of that delightful subject. In the explanations, the effort has been to lead the young student to reason for himself and to develop his individual taste. With this object the illustrations are selected rather as types, and certain characteristics of national styles of ornament are touched upon in such a way as to indicate a plan for systematic study.

A further object I have had before me has been to help the young craftsman, and those responsible for the development of young minds, to ennoble and refine everything on which their influences may be brought to bear, and so to find greater delight in the improvement of their surroundings.

Let the words of Ruskin be borne in mind :

" Design is not the offspring of idle fancy ; it is the studied result of accumulative observation and delightful habit."

I wish to thank Mr. Walter Crane for giving me permission to reproduce his plate of the marsh marigold. It is most valuable, as showing how to make a study from Nature for decorative purposes. I am indebted also to Mr. Richard Glazier for the study of the clematis, and my thanks are due to the authorities of the British Museum for affording me facilities for the study of the prehistoric forms (Plate VIII.), and for permission to include the manuscripts from the excellent series of reproductions issued by that institution.

HENRY CADNESS.

Didsbury, Manchester,
    March, 1902.

CONTENTS.

CONTENTS.

DECORATIVE BRUSH-WORK
& ELEMENTARY DESIGN.

CHAPTER I.

MATERIALS, ETC.

OBJECT IN DESIGNING.

A DESIGN may be described as a set of definite instructions in line, colour, or relief, made for the guidance of the craftsman in the production of an object of use or of beauty. Nothing vague or doubtful, therefore, will be admissible.

Such a design will necessarily be free of any attempts to imitate the qualities of the materials to be employed, but in its conception the designer will have calculated on certain effects natural to the material; thus his design is only a means to an end. Whether for buildings, furniture, pottery, or surface decoration, such as textiles or wall-papers, the design will clearly show the intention, and where necessary will be supplemented by written dimensions, "colour notes," and sections showing the projections of mouldings and other parts in relief.

In order to obtain or convey an idea of any complete object, it is usual to make an "effect" sketch on a small scale, and of a pictorial kind ; of a solid object, a perspective sketch as it would appear from a certain point of view ; and of a repeating pattern, one in colour showing the effect of repeating the units of the design. So a distinction between the production of a picture and of a design is obvious—the one is a complete permanent thing, the other only temporary.

MATERIALS USED IN DESIGNING.

To ensure definition in a design, it is advisable to draw on paper which has a smooth surface. "Strong cartridge" which is generally used, is sold in sheets and in rolls, the latter up to 20 yards in length and 60 inches wide. For large cartoons this is best and cheapest, averaging 9d. per yard. For small work, unruled foolscap writing paper, and even ordinary note paper answers very well, whilst for pen-and-ink drawings "Bristol" or "London" board, or white millboard is often used ; the thicker qualities of these will take either tempera or transparent water colours readily.

"Lining" paper is very useful for working drawings and for charcoal demonstrations. It is sold in rolls for paperhangers' use.

Tinted crayon papers, smooth and unglazed, are frequently used when a coloured ground is required, and will be found economical and effective ; the colour is in the pulp of the paper and not on the surface only, as in grounded papers. Thirty or forty different tints are made. A good quality of smooth, unglazed, brown parcel paper, if not absorbent, is very useful for large studies ; purchased by the roll it forms an excellent substitute for a blackboard. and is most valuable for working drawings. Grounded wall-papers, without pattern, can be purchased in many colours ; the " sanitary " grounded papers being prepared with a water resisting surface, will take either water or oil colours, and are very useful for permanent decorations, such as door panels and friezes.

Generally the designer "lays" his own grounds, as it is seldom possible to purchase the exact tint required ; and, further, alterations are easily made by using the ground colour for painting out.

Papers having a toothed or grain surface, thick and partly absorbent, are used by the picture painters, the roughness helping to produce varied effects, and the strength of the paper allowing of blotting, sponging and dragging the colours, so as to suggest the mystery and gradation which have such a charm in Nature, and are so much appreciated by the artist. Such papers are made in great variety, each having qualities preferred by different individuals, and for different kinds of work.

Whatman's " rough," " medium " or " not," and "hot pressed" are terms used to describe three grades of surfaces ; the two first are descriptive, the third points to the smoothing of the surface by pressure between hot cylinders.

Generally white or cream paper is used for transparent water-colour painting, the reflection of light through the colour giving a luminous quality, which is impossible to obtain by any other means.

Sugar paper, packing paper, and other make-shifts are not to be recommended for early practice, as the manipulation of form and colour presents sufficient difficulties, without those peculiar to such materials ; but in the hands of a practised worker they can be put to good use. Some colour effects are possible only on such grounds, their roughness and absorbent properties being favourable. Rice paper, used by the Japanese artists, is absorbent, the colours soaking into the paper and giving a beautiful soft effect, as seen in their wood-block printing.

A blackboard is useful for large work, not only for rapid sketches, but for setting out full size large designs in mass, with chalk, from which careful detailed tracings can be made for transfer to the drawing paper.

A plate of ground glass, framed and backed with black, gives a grey ground of a perfect surface for white chalk and charcoal sketching, and if backed with white it is excellent for black or colour work.

A substitute of a cheap and portable nature can be made of American morocco cloth, dull surface, pinned on to a frame, or even the wall. It can be rolled up, thus enabling drawings which are worked in tempera or chalk to be retained and stored for future use, so that a set of charts or diagrams for comparative lessons can be collected at a small cost; and, if fixed with shellac as described later, or painted in oil colour, these will be quite permanent.

"Satteen," a smooth-faced cotton fabric, is also useful for diagrams worked in tempera colour. This fabric is dyed in a variety of beautiful colours, and with a little practice is easily worked on. For festival and other temporary purposes, beautiful effects are obtainable.

Tracing cloth, semi-transparent, readily takes Indian ink or transparent water, or oil colours, giving effects useful for window screens and blinds, the transmitted light can be utilised for the display of teaching diagrams, or in decoration.

Paper, such as cartridge, pasted with starch or flour paste on linen or cotton, is most serviceable for cartoon or working drawings which have much handling.

Brown holland, stretched on a frame, and coated with size until it is rendered non-porous, gives another ground useful for large work. On this transparent oil colours can be used, and, with a transmitted light, they give beautiful effects. The same material, or, for large scenes, a coarse canvas, when coated with size to which whiting is added, gives the opaque canvas on which the scene-painter produces his effects with tempera colour.

"Michelet" and "Canzon" are French toned papers, useful for bold work, the former having an effective parallel grain.

For highly finished drawings it is best to strain the paper, so as to have a flat even surface, that will not "cockle" when colour is applied. To do this, damp the paper all over the back, having previously turned the edges up about half an inch all round. Wipe this edge, or the excess of moisture will dilute the glue or paste, which must be next applied to the edges. Place on the drawing board, and press the edges into close contact. Keep under pressure with another board until it adheres firmly, and is dry.

The face side of the paper is that on which the watermark reads rightly when held up to the light, or that side on which the web texture is not so distinct.

To strain on linen, coat the paper all over with starch, and press closely on a stretched sheet of fine linen or cotton fabric until dry.

Stretching frames are made, to fit accurately over a drawing board, or another frame. The paper is cut larger than the inner frame or board, and, when wetted, the stretching frame is fitted over the edges and secured at the back with clips ; something like a child's transparent drawing slate.

In straining, the paper expands with the moisture, and in drying endeavours to return to its original size, but the cemented or gripped edges prevent this, and a tightly strained paper is the result.

In water-colour painting, some effects are best produced by working on moist paper. To accomplish this a light frame is covered with linen, and the paper strained over it, so that the paper and the linen can be wetted at the back, thus preventing the colour from drying quickly. This rapid drying presents great difficulties to the beginner, especially in hot weather. Another simple and convenient way of keeping the paper moist is to use a waterproof portfolio to contain the dry paper and sketches. Place a sheet of wet blotting paper on the cover, and the moistened drawing paper when laid on this adheres by suction. As the moisture evaporates, it is replaced by more, applied to the edges of the blotting paper. By the way, atmospheric conditions affect the drying of water-colours so much, that on a moist day, or a dewy evening the paper will remain wet for hours.

DRY MATERIALS.

The materials used for expressing form may be divided into three classes—(1) those of a friable nature applied by friction, (2) those used in a liquid state and applied with brush or pen, and (3) those in which a plastic material is applied, as in modelling, or in which the ground is cut away, as in carving. In the first class, charcoal is the most primitive. It is applied or removed readily ; tone or shaded drawings are produced by rubbing with the finger or leather stump, and erasures made with chamois leather, India rubber, or new bread kneaded to a point.   Willow and vine twigs, free from knots, are charred and sold ready for use.   Like many other useful things, charcoal is liable to abuse, and nothing will hinder the student and induce bad habits more than slovenly use of this material.   In careful hands it is light in shade, silvery, transparent, hopeful ; in careless hands it is dirt, blackness, and despair. Hence some eminent men do not advise its use by the beginner.   If blackness arises in the working, it can be lessened by blowing briskly, as the charcoal lies lightly until fixed.

Black chalk, conté crayon, and carbon pencil have properties similar to charcoal, but they adhere more firmly.   They are made in different degrees of hardness, mounted in wood like blacklead pencil ; the chalk is also sold in a powder for applying with stumps or the finger, and has been the chief medium for shading in schools.   The remarks on abuse of charcoal apply equally to these.

The absence of gloss and freedom in working have led to a preference for these in preparing large drawings.

For fine outline and silvery shading the black-lead pencil has been mostly employed. The convenient form in which it is sold, and its " silky " quality in use, especially on smooth paper, adhering, yet easily erased with India rubber, account for this. It is possible to obtain tones * of rich full black, or of the most delicate silvery greys, according to the hardness or softness of the pencil. Generally the rougher the paper, the harder the pencil may be, and in any case it is best not to force the material, as in the deep tones a disagreeable polish is sometimes produced. A pencil of good quality is cheapest in the end ; it cuts better, is free from grit, and does not stain the paper.

These materials do not adhere very firmly to the paper, and are therefore useful for transferring with. Coloured chalks are used for similar

* TONE.—The relative strength of dark or light apart from *colour* or *tint.* Thus a blue may be as strong in *tone* as a red, or it may be of a lighter or darker *tone.*

TINT.—Degrees of strength of any one colour, usually referring to paler or diluted colour. Thus one rose may be crimson, another a pale *tint* pink.

SHADE.—Interrupted light deepening the tones and neutralising colours. Thus a pale blue is not only less light in the shade portion, but the blue is deadened.

HUE.—Relates to the result of mixing two colours, as blue and yellow make a green, which may be bluer or yellower in hue as the case may be.

purposes ; the " sanguine," a red chalk, gives the colour so much used by the old masters.

On dark grounds white chalk is useful, and on brown paper rapid effects of light and shade, or of tone decorations, are easily produced, with chalk for the lights and charcoal for the shades, preserving much of the brown ground for half-tone.

Sometimes a tone of charcoal is rubbed evenly over a sheet of white paper, the lights being picked out with India rubber, and the shades added with charcoal.

If white chalk and charcoal are used, they should not be allowed to mix, as they produce a disagreeable grey.

White chalks, stained with liquid dyes and dried, are very useful for temporary colour effects and blackboard work.

Drawings made with these materials can be rendered permanent, by fixing or spraying over them, by means of a scent diffuser, a solution of white shellac* in spirits of wine, lightly at first and allowing to dry, and repeating the spraying until fixed. Too much fixing will give a glossy surface ; the spirit evaporates, leaving the shellac to bind the chalk. If necessary, a drawing thus fixed can be worked on in chalks or water colour, and fixed again. Milk, gum-water, and hot water washed

* FIXATIVE.—Dissolve 1 oz. of white shellac in about 6 ozs. of methylated spirit : pour from the sediment, and use.

over are also used to fix, but they are liable to disturb the drawing.

Wax chalks, of great variety of colours, are very convenient to use on toned or white paper, especially for note books or diagrams. They require no fixing, as the wax in their composition gives sufficient adhesion. They are sold encased in wood like blacklead pencils, and in solid sticks; the latter are most useful for large work.

All the foregoing are applied to the paper by pressure and in a dry form, and are considerably limited in range of tone and colour.

LIQUID MATERIALS.

Water colours give a much greater range, and are generally preferred for designing. The modern convenient form in which they are supplied gives the greatest facilities. Briefly, water colours are purified pigments of an earthy, metallic, animal, or vegetable origin, carefully ground with water to a fine paste. If applied to the paper in this state, the colour will be in the form of a loose powder when the water has evaporated; therefore it is necessary to add some adhesive matter, which will bind the colour to the surface.

Gum arabic, a vegetable product, is one of the best. It is easily dissolved in water, and does not discolour. It should be mixed fresh in cold water to the consistency of thin cream; the ready-made

gums, so useful for office purposes, often contain
preservatives which injure the colours.   Sugar,
honey, and glycerine are added, to keep the colour
in a moist state, but, as these have the property of
absorbing moisture from the atmosphere, they do
not dry as hard as the pure gum.   This property
can be turned to good use in picture painting,
when gradations and broken colour are required;
but an excess will be found disagreeably sticky
and pasty.

Size, or a weak solution of glue, an animal
matter, is largely used for decoration, but its consistency changes with the temperature, it is liable
to coagulate in cold weather, and in hot will decom-
pose and smell badly.   The terms " tempera " and
" distemper " are given to mixtures of this kind, it
is said, because of the latter property and their
unglazed surface.   The colours used in wall-paper
printing and in decorative painting are frequently
mixed with size, and are sometimes used slightly
warm.

Colours mixed with white of egg (albumen), to
which a little vinegar is added, or with the yolk,
adhere very firmly, gaining in hardness with time
and when thinly varnished are of great per-
manence.   The tempera paintings of the early
Italian period, previous to the introduction of oil
colours, were executed with this medium, and
they are of the purest colour, of a dull surface,
rich and luminous.

Generally these water mixtures will not bear much handling, the hardness depending chiefly on soluble materials, which do not undergo much change in drying. Nevertheless, they form the chief and most valuable materials for indoor decoration and for the designer's general use.

Pigments mixed with oils and resinous varnishes are used for decorative painting, and for pictorial work. The oils undergo a chemical change, in which the atmosphere plays a great part, rendering the colour practically insoluble, extremely hard and durable. These are seldom used for designs, except for diagrams and outdoor work.

Oil colour usually dries with a glossy surface; but by thinning the colour with paraffin a dull surface is produced. Japanners' gold size, mixed with pigment, gives a quick-drying, hard colour; thinned with turpentine it is largely used in decorative work.

Naphtha and spirit colours, and varnish stains give another class of colours which dry rapidly. Shellac dissolved in spirits of wine forms the medium, and lacquers come under the same heading. French polish, or spirit varnish, with pigments added, makes a quick-drying colour, useful for diagrams and for temporary decoration and it can be used outdoors.

Pigments may be divided into two classes: the transparent and the opaque. The former, such as Crimson lake, Indian yellow, Prussian blue, etc.,

require a light ground, on which they are painted
thickly or thinly, more or less diluted with water,
in order to obtain dark or light tones. It is
obvious that pure tints of a transparent pigment
can only be obtained on white paper; for instance,
on a cream-coloured paper, a pale wash of blue
will become greenish in hue, and purple will become
browned by the yellow of the paper showing
through it.

Transparent pigments yield the most charming
gradations of colour, so that even accidental blots
have a certain beauty; and the liquid effects of
broken colour, so fascinating in Turner's landscapes,
show the value of such pigments in the hands of
a master.

It is seldom that these variations are used in
a design, because such qualities are almost impossible to reproduce in the materials worked
from the designs. Perhaps in enamel and pottery
painting we can surpass them in richness and
intensity, properties peculiar to vitrified and other
glazed colours. We must not be tempted, for the
sake of a beautiful "show" drawing, to neglect
the practical side.

Opaque pigments, such as chrome yellow,
vermilion, ochre, and others, are most valuable
for painting on coloured grounds, their solidity
serving to obliterate the ground on which they
are placed, and so to present them in their purity
and flatness without gradations.

Plate II.

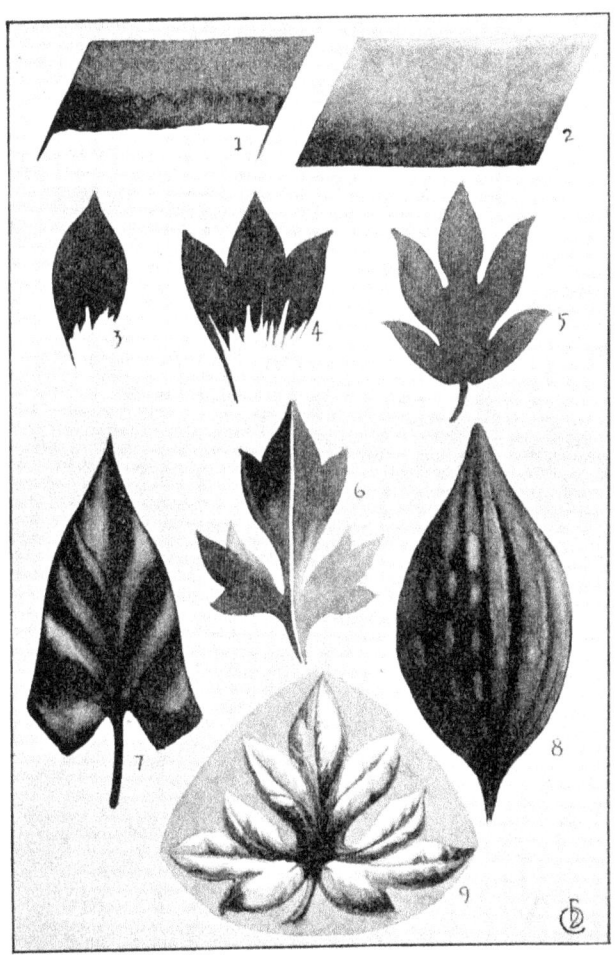

WASH EFFECTS WITH TRANSPARENT WATER-COLOUR.

By the addition of white the transparent colours are made opaque, and at the same time paler in colour and somewhat greyer in tint. For instance, Vandyke brown gives a rich warm colour as a transparent wash, but it becomes purply when white is added. Many other colours also lose in richness in the same way. The greyness can be somewhat counteracted by the addition of a little yellow.

Generally it is best to apply the opaque colours solidly, though, if too thick, they are likely to crack away from the paper. If used of about the same consistency as cream, they will dry perfectly flat; but if too liquid the colours of the lightest weight will separate and float, the heaviest sinking, and so quite frustrating the intention of having a definite colour.

Transparent colour, on the contrary, is used quite liquid, and flat tints are laid by allowing the colour to gravitate (Plate II., figs. 1 to 4). The paper being inclined, the artist leads the colour to the shapes required and picks off portions of colour whilst moist with blotting paper and brush, (Plate II., figs. 7 and 8), and dilutes the colour for paler tones and gradations (Plate II., fig. 6).

In oil paintings as well as tempera, the colours are used thick and pasty, so that they will keep the shapes and positions they are placed in.

To obtain rich effects on tinted grounds it is necessary to paint the objects in silhouette with white or other opaque pigments, and when this is quite dry, to overpaint with transparent colours. Thus, white may have a delicate purple painted over it, or vermilion, used as a foundation, might have Crimson lake or other transparent colour superimposed, which would give the utmost richness and depth.

It is very important to have sufficient gum or size in the pigment to make it adhere firmly. When dry, it should be hard enough to bear brisk rubbing with the finger; if there is not sufficient, the colour will be partly absorbent, and will be difficult to work on with subsequent paintings. On the other hand, too much gum or size will cause the colour to crack, besides making it less opaque. Experiments only will enable the student to make it just right.

The ordinary tubes or pans of moist colour, with or without Chinese white, are best for water-colour work, as they are prepared with great care, and, by using Chinese white, they will answer well for tempera painting ; but for this purpose, where colour is wanted in large quantities, it will be more economical to use powder colours, grinding them on a glass slab (Plate III., fig. 2), with a muller (fig. 1), and palette knife (fig. 3). Whilst grinding keep the colour in a pasty state with water, grinding a little only at a time until it is very fine, and placing it in a cover pot (fig. 6), taking a little more until all is fine. The gum may be added whilst grinding ; if afterwards, it will tend to deepen

Plate III.

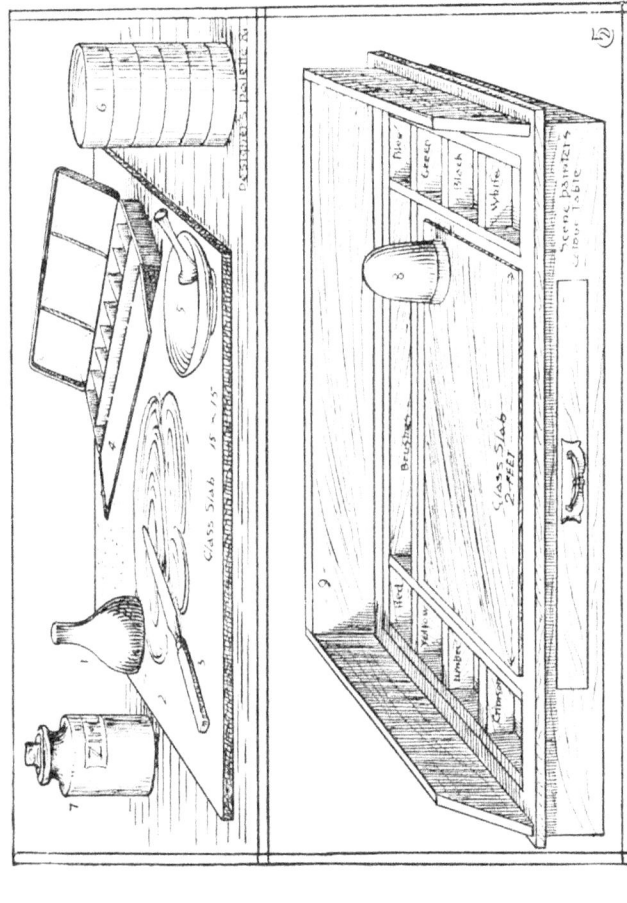

DESIGNER'S AND SCENE PAINTER'S COLOUR TABLES, PALETTE, ETC.

the tone, and if any particles of colour are not
completely levigated they will affect the batch
of colour in working. So, in this as in everything,
care and completeness in each stage will prevent
disappointments later. It must be borne in mind
that the water alone evaporates from the colour,
so that in thinning the colour afterwards, water
only should be used.

The ordinary water colours can be mixed with
the tempera ones, so that small quantities can be
made without much trouble.

A box to contain eight moist colours (Plate III.,
fig. 4) should be obtained, and should be filled
with colours as required, beginning with three
only, and using them until familiar with their
characteristics. Crimson lake, Prussian blue, and
Indian yellow, although not absolutely permanent,
yet will provide innumerable tints, excellent for
first practice.

Besides water colours there are inks and stains
obtainable which are most useful for demonstration,
working drawings, and designs. Indian ink, indelible brown, and Prout's brown, are very useful
for outlining ; some of these, when dry, take washes
of colour without being disturbed.

Waterproof drawing inks are useful for large flat
washes, such as may be required for architectural
work and for diagrams, the Indian ink being
especially good for black-and-white work for reproduction as book illustrations. So indelible is it, that

a pale photographic print can be penned over with
it, and when the photograph is bleached the lines
remain.   Thus many line drawings are produced
for the purpose of making printing blocks.

Stains mixed in water, such as are sold for wood
work, are very useful for line drawing and for brush
work.   Oak, walnut, and ebony, are perfect for the
purpose, and will be found economical for large
work, such as cartoons, and for book illustrations ;
also for pen-and-ink and school brush-drawing
Stephens' " ebony stain" is excellent; the ordinary
writing inks being less black and wanting in
density.

Zinc white with a little gum arabic makes a
beautiful white paint, valuable for similar purposes
on dark paper, and a thorough grinding on a glass
slab makes the colour more opaque.   It should be
kept ready for use in a stoppered bottle (Plate III.,
fig. 7).

For the workshop or large classes a table
arranged, as on Plate III., fig. 9, will be most
convenient.

Pulp colours, such as scene painters use, can be
purchased ready ground with water, requiring gum
or size only.

TOOLS.

For applying liquid colours, pens of steel or quill,
or brushes of sable, ox, camel, or hog hair are used.

The character of the work depends more on the

tools than the old saw justifies. "A bad workman blames his tools," no doubt, but a good workman does better work with good tools, and the better care he takes of them.

Sable and camel hair have the property of clinging together when wet, and, if the natural tips of hair are used, the finest point can be produced. On the trimming of the hairs depends the fineness of the point, and it is not always the smallest brush that is the finest.

In various handicrafts the brushes are trimmed differently. In litho drawing, where a pen would scratch the prepared paper, the brush is used, and sometimes cut at the sides until only a few hairs remain (Plate IV., fig. 28), giving a line of the utmost fineness. Glass and pottery painters use "writers" or "riggers" (fig. 12), so called because used for lettering signs or the rigging of ships in pictures, or "tracers" which give the full flow of colour necessary to stand the firing in the kiln. This make of brush is excellent where uniform thickness of line is required, and especially when the end is blunted by cutting (fig. 14), or, better still, when worn by careful using.

For gradated strokes, or broad spaces of colour, a "goose quill" of sable (Plate IV., fig. 9) will be most generally useful ; this hair is more flexible than camel hair, and with it the greatest variety of shapes can be made.

Similar round brushes are made, mounted in

metal; but quills are preferable, as they are not so tightly bound. The pressure of the metal tends to cause the hairs to spread like a mop, while with careful use the quills will not split.

Swan quill, duck, goose, and so on, express the different sizes, whilst in metal, numbers are used. Nos. 6 and 7 are about goose-quill size.

Flat water-colour brushes (Plate IV., fig. 17) are sold in metal mounts, and are useful for lettering and lining, the broad side of the brush giving thick down strokes, and the narrow edge the thinner lines, much in the same way as the quill pen is used in lettering (Plate IV., fig. 19).

Flat brushes of hog hair are useful for laying grounds of tempera colour; the stiff hair giving greater control than the flexible camel or sable hair (Plate IV., figs. 3, 4, 7).

Japanese brushes (Plate IV., figs. 23 to 26) are perfectly adapted for drawing or writing, the shapes being selected for the particular work in hand. These brushes are mounted in bamboo, and are held vertically, between the first and second fingers of the right hand, so that the point is perfectly under control.

The learner will soon discover that a soft-haired brush cannot be pushed without the hairs turning back. Generally it is best to hold the brush between the finger and thumb, as in using a pen, but nearly upright, and slanting a little in the direction it is to be drawn; thus the hairs will be kept to a point.

Plate IV.

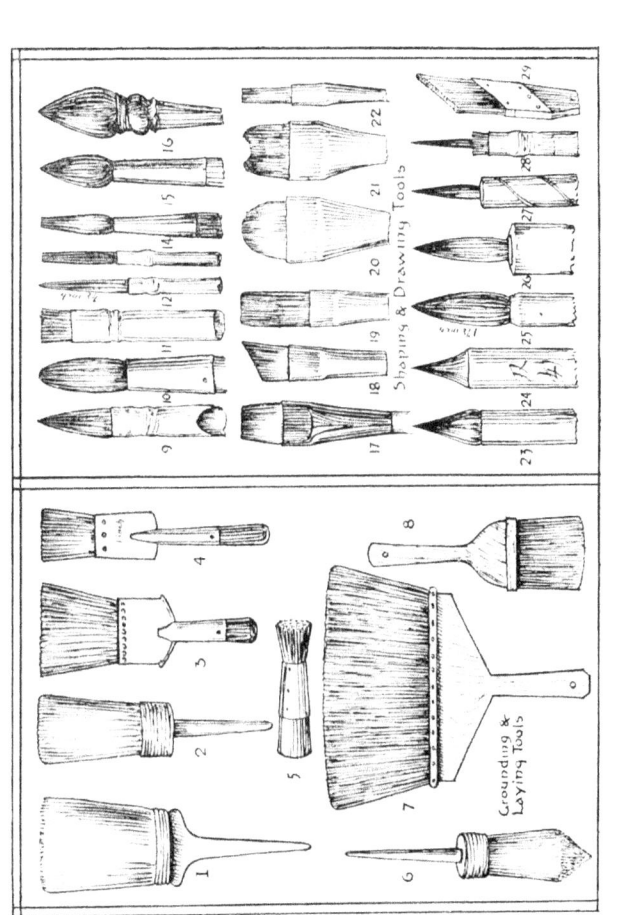

Shaping & Drawing Tools

Grounding & Laying Tools

BRUSHES USED IN DESIGNING AND BRUSH WORK.

Figs. 1, 2, 6, and 8, on Plate IV., are best for covering large grounds, and figs. 20 and 21 are worn brushes, useful for landscape painting.

The pen is universally employed in Europe for writing with liquid colour, and for drawing where lines of somewhat equal thickness are desirable; fine or coarse according to the hardness or shape of its point.

Quill pens are the most sympathetic, and can be trimmed as required, giving a crisp line when newly cut, and a softer line when worn. The quality of line renders it peculiarly suitable for lettering, and Gothic lettering is very expressive of the pen influence.

Reed pens, formed of reed or bamboo cane, are very useful for larger work; these and quills do not cut the paper like metal pens, and bolder work is possible with them.

Metal pens are generally used for fine drawing, especially for drawings which are to be reproduced by printing processes. They have the advantage of uniformity, and are ready for constant use. For strong lines some double pens are useful. " The Flying Dutchman " and "The Camel " are somewhat of the reservoir type, and do not require so frequent dipping, an important point in rapid working. " Crow-quill " pens are used for the finest work. It must be remembered that metal pens are liable to cut and destroy the surface of the paper, hence the lithographer works with a fine brush instead, and Japanese paper is so soft as to render the use of a hard pen impossible. Fountain pens are very useful for sketching, especially if a dense black ink can be used, but generally such ink does not flow freely from their delicate mechanism.

For "line process"—*i.e.*, for reproduction as a printing block by the aid of photography—it is necessary to draw with a clear black line and a crisp touch, as grey and woolly lines will not stand the process. Shades and tones must be rendered by lines placed close together, or crossing each other ("cross-hatching"), and just as in handwriting every individual has his characteristics, so in pen drawing the treatment depends on the individual. Albert Durer preferred lines following the contours, making every touch help to express the surface or texture, and using very little cross-hatching in most of his illustrations. This treatment was particularly helpful to the wood engraver, as it allowed clear cutting and vigorous lines, whilst in etching, cross-hatching was used for varying the tones and the production of soft effects, by different depths of etching and of the transparent ink employed.

Daniel Vierge, Phil May, and others show great economy in the use of lines applied to different subjects, and with very different but beautiful results. The student will learn much by copying portions of such masterly work very carefully, with the object of understanding the economical use of

lines and the very simple way of expressing effects
—lines parallel, crossed, spotting, and even the
splashing of ink from a stiff brush, being turned to
account.

CHAPTER II.

PREPARATORY WORK.

WORKING DRAWINGS.

IN practical designing, the drawing or sketch, as
already stated, will give definite instructions to the
craftsman, leaving nothing to chance. It is obvious
that when the design is for solid objects, such as
vases, caskets, etc., modelling in wax or clay, if
only on a small scale, will help to realise the effects
of different planes. In some crafts, working drawings are made on a much larger scale than the final
material. In weaving, for instance, carpets are drawn
the same size as the cloth, whilst silks are frequently
designed seven or eight times the size of the cloth.
Such working drawings are made expressly to guide
the worker in his arrangements of threads, and
would, on a smaller scale, be confusing. Plate V.,
figs. 1 and 2, give a leaf repeat together with the
cloth size sketch. Again, for minute work, as in pen
illustrations, large designs are made so as to bear
reduction by photography. In any case the designer

Plate V.

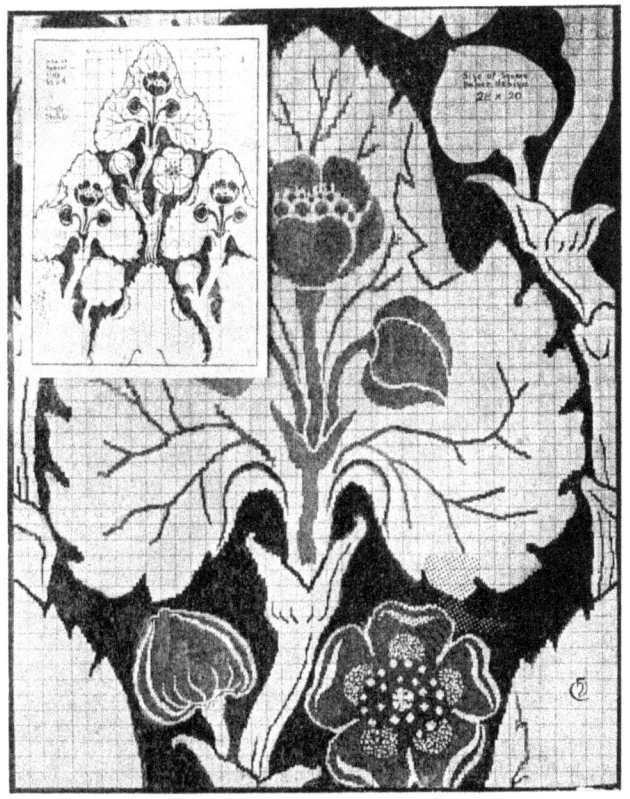

EFFECT SKETCH AND WORKING DRAWING FOR A WOVEN FABRIC.

calculates on the reduction yielding the desired effect, and by viewing the large drawing through a concave reducing glass, or a reversed opera glass, some idea of the final result will be gained.

Generally, the colouring of such enlargements is only symbolic, as in weaving, where vermilion and ultramarine are used for their distinctness in indicating the relative rising and falling of the warp threads. Burnt sienna, Raw sienna, Prussian blue, Olive green are also useful for this purpose, and are not so crude, the squared paper lines being easily counted through such colours. By the way, most working drawings for weaving are carried out on paper ruled in squares of 6 × 8, or 8 × 8, or other divisions of the half-inch squares, in order to facilitate counting the threads and cutting the cards.

In some handicrafts, such as repousse and other metal work, embroidery, enamel, etc., points will arise whilst working in the material, which may suggest modifications of the details. So the expert craftsman, preparing his own design, will omit them in the drawing, or only indicate those easily produced. Thus the original intention may be departed from, in order to embody some of the beautiful qualities inherent in the material and from an apparently meagre drawing an object will be produced, in which the plain parts become beautified, as in embroidery where the stitches, impossible to express fully in a drawing, become a primary feature in the final effect, and so in other cases (Plate VI., figs. 1, 2, 3, and 4).

It may be stated broadly that a design is unsatisfactory which does not turn such properties to the best use, neither obscuring by superabundance of detail (pretty only on paper), nor straining to make one material imitate another; each has its beauties, they may be rough or smooth, soft or hard, rich or delicate, and these qualities should always have full consideration.

The small scale sketch will be best executed with the brush and colour, carefully indicating the distribution of the primary masses of pattern and the constructive lines. A better result is ensured if this sketch also includes the surroundings; for example, a panel in a door will be but part of a whole scheme, a stained window or wrought-iron gate will have architectural surroundings, with which they must harmonise, and a small sketch may obviate anything incongruous. Such scale sketches are usually about 1 inch to a foot, or in repeating patterns about $2\frac{1}{2}$ inches to a foot. This latter is useful for testing repeating patterns, of which four repeats at least should be indicated, the details being omitted. Of course, small patterns such as dress fabrics, will be tested full size. Plate VII., figs. 6 and 7, gives some idea of such sketches.

When the scheme is settled in the form of a scale sketch, an enlargement is made to full size. This is effected by ruling an equal number of

Plate VI.

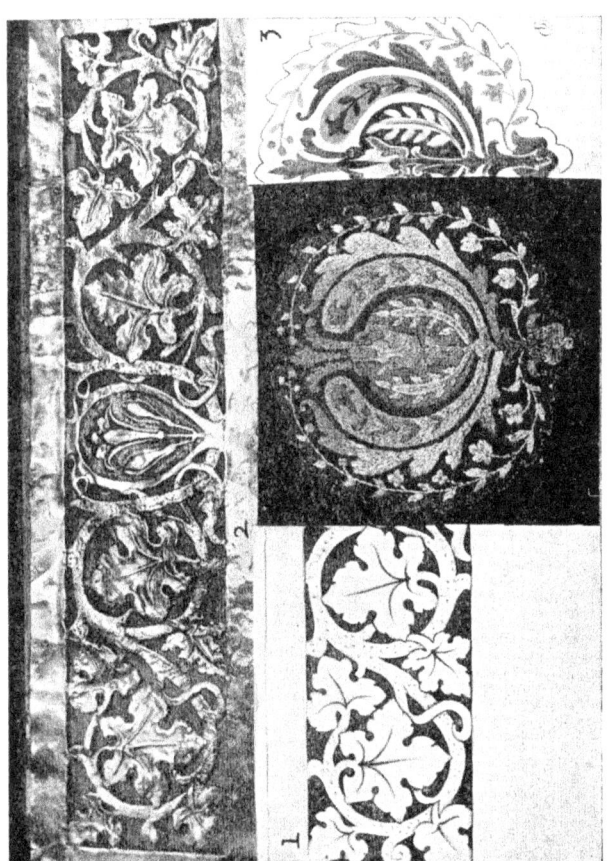

WORKING DRAWINGS FOR EMBROIDERY AND PIERCED RAISED COPPER, AND
SPECIMENS IN THE MATERIAL.

Plate VII.

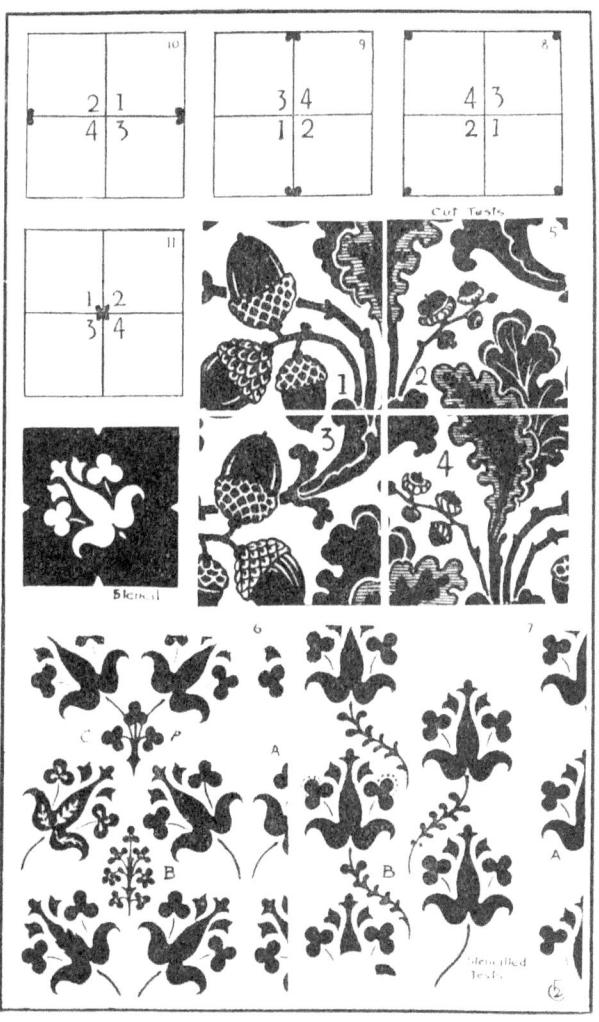

METHODS OF TESTING REPEATING PATTERNS.

dividing lines on the large paper and on the sketch, and where the pattern is intersected by these lines we find corresponding points on the enlarged squares, and draw through them (Plate V., figs. 1 and 2). This will ensure accuracy of position and proportion of the large masses, the details being added afterwards.

In large repeating patterns, only one repeat needs to be enlarged, if the sketch is accurate, though it will be best to test the enlargement also. There are various ways of doing this. By cutting the pattern into four parts and transposing to form other centres (Plate VII., figs. 5, 8, 9, 10, and 11), it is possible to correct the joinings and centrings, and so ensure the avoidance of ugly stripes of either ground or pattern.

Another method is to stencil four or six repeats broadly in tempera colour. This is a certain way, and is not difficult to do (Plate VII., figs. 6 and 7). A description of the process is given on page 42.

The transfer of drawings may be effected in many ways. The simplest is to place the pencilled drawing face downwards on the surface on which it is to be worked, and rubbing the back firmly with the thumb nail or a smooth knife handle. Placing a piece of thin paper on the back of the drawing to receive the friction, will prevent it from being torn or distorted. Tracings made with a soft pencil, say HB, on strong tracing paper, will yield as many as a dozen transfers, all clean and sharp and ready for painting. It will be noticed that a reversed pattern will result, and if lettering is used it will read backwards, so that it becomes necessary to re-pencil the design on the back before transferring it. Frequent pencilling tends to destroy the vigour and character of a drawing, and it must be remembered that hurried careless work will transfer with all its defects, and give endless trouble in painting.

By placing carbon paper (such as is used for office purposes) between the drawing and the final sheet and pencilling over the lines, a transfer is obtained, but each transfer requires special pencilling. To prevent the drawing from being damaged, place a piece of tracing paper over it each time, to receive the pencilling, and take care not to cut through with the pencil or the stylus. Carbon paper is usually of an oily nature, therefore it is best to prepare a sheet of thin paper with blacklead, Indian red, or other dry colour, in any case rubbing the colour well into the paper, so that it will not smear. Paper treated in this way with white chalk answers very well for transfers on a dark ground. Chalk or powder colour, rubbed well into the back of the drawing, will transfer readily in this way.

Another way is by painting a fine brush outline on tracing paper placed over the drawing, using zinc white mixed with water only, to a creamy consistency, without any adhesive matter. When dry the colour will leave the paper readily by pressure on the back. By using dark powder colours in this way transfers can be made on canvas, linen, silk, etc., for embroidery.

The process of " pouncing " is useful for transferring to surfaces which will not bear much rubbing. The pattern is drawn on smooth tough paper (tracing paper will do), and then pierced with a needle. Through the perforations a fine powder is then dusted and rubbed with cotton wool, felt, or, better still, a fine muslin bag containing the powder. With practice the perforations are made very quickly and evenly, and, if two or three pieces of paper are placed under the pattern, duplicates can be pierced at the same time. A piece of fine baize or cloth should be put under the pattern whilst piercing it. The advantage in using a perforated pattern is that many transfers can be taken from it, and in crafts, such as glass and pottery painting, and house decoration, it is preferred. Charcoal, chalk, and dry colour can be used in this way ; whilst for embroidery, powder to which a little resin is added will give a fixed transfer if a hot iron is passed over a sheet of blotting paper placed upon the pounced cloth.

Modifications of these processes are made to suit circumstances. Folding a pattern down the centre and piercing, will give a bi-symmetrical pattern. In one half the perforations will not catch the powder well, but rubbing the burr on the back of the tracing with fine sandpaper, will cause the pattern to work freely.

It will occur to the student that a mirror (unframed) placed on its edge will serve to test half a symmetrical pattern, and that two mirrors placed on the outer edges of a pattern will repeat it indefinitely, or if placed at right angles will test a multi-symmetrical pattern, such as a cornered tile or a diaper repeat.

An arrangement of lenses for repeating and enlarging, which forms the subject of a patent, should be of great use in testing designs unsymmetrical as well as symmetrical.

In setting out patterns on large surfaces, a string of cotton or worsted, rubbed with chalk or charcoal and "struck" while the ends are held tightly, will give a line which can easily be removed after the decoration is finished.

STENCILLING.

Stencilling may be described as a process midway between mechanical and hand work, as the design is cut out in paper or thin metal plates, through which it is afterwards painted or powdered on to the required surface, thus affording a simple means of repeating a design economically. For wall decoration it has been used since Pompeiian times, and previous to the use of paperhangings it was the usual means of decorating walls which were not draped. In Japan this process is commonly used for decorating fabrics, lacquer, and paper, and in modern pottery a thick paper stencil is used for impressing a sunk ground or pattern to receive glazes. Even plastering and gesso are applied in low relief by means of wooden stencils, which in many respects are like fret-work patterns.

For colour work, waterproof tough paper is used. " Willesden paper " answers well, and tin-foil or lead-foil are good for brushing over, as they lie very closely to the surface being decorated.

For general use try cartridge paper, coated all over on both sides with " patent knotting " (a preparation of shellac to be obtained at any paint stores), applied with a hog-hair brush ; or drawing paper, coated with linseed oil, which makes it transparent, so that it can be placed over the drawing which it is desired to trace. This oil paper takes two or three weeks to dry; knotting dries in an hour. When the design is traced on to the waterproof paper, it is cut with a sharp-pointed knife, on a plate of glass, as the grain of a wooden surface would not permit of accurate cutting. The cutting must be clean and well into the corners, so that the pieces come away without tearing. Punches are used when many small circles are required.

Japanese stencils are cut on thin paper, many layers together. Ties are made to form part of the

design (Plate XX., fig. 8), and detached pieces
and weak parts of the stencil are kept in position
by cementing hair, or silk threads across to the
stronger parts; these are so fine that the colour
works under them, and they are not visible in the
final work.

Flat-ended hog-hair brushes (Plate IV., fig. 5), are
used to "dabble" the colour through the perforations. If brushed across, the edges of the pattern
catch the colour and this causes blots and smears.
The dabbling gives a texture quite different from
that of brush working, and is capable of an
infinite variety of gradations and colour blendings,
of the softest and most harmonious quality. A
soft sponge can also be used for this purpose.

The ground or the pattern can be cut away,
or, by using two stencils, the outline can be left,
or a secondary pattern introduced; and by using
more stencils still greater variations are possible;
but in this, as in all decoration, simplicity will be
found best.

The necessity for ties or bonds across parts of
the patterns compel care in designing, and wherever
possible the ties should play a part in the pattern,
so that there may be no necessity for painting
them out, as the economy of the process is
minimised by any hand touching afterwards.

Pierced metal work is really a stencil treatment.
Plate VI., fig. 2, shows this, the ground being cut
away instead of the pattern.

The colours may be tempera, oil, or water colour, but they must be kept of a consistency such as will not run under the stencil plate.

If the paper for a finished drawing has been strained, the transfer can be made directly, if the white ground is to play a part in the effect. If the ground is to be tinted, the tint should be laid before the transfer is made, as, if it is put on afterwards, the colour will fix the transfer and render any alterations difficult.

Transparent water colour can be floated on, as explained on page 17, or tempera colour laid with a flat hog-hair brush, crossing and re-crossing the paper, so as to spread the colour evenly and when dry the paper will strain flat again, and the colour will dry evenly.

It is possible to adapt this ground-laying effectively and economically for panels and borders such as are seen in illuminated manuscripts, by using flat paper masks, cut to the size and shape of the border required. This is really a kind of stencilling on which the finer details can be worked.

CHAPTER III.

METHODS OF EXPRESSION.

FREEDOM in drawing and expressing form is absolutely necessary in designing. With this object, exercises in proportion and precision are given in the elementary stage of school work, both the pencil and pen being used to express areas and contours. There has been much controversy on this subject, freehand drawing in the schools being attacked. One reason against it being that there is no outline in Nature. Certainly there is no line bounding solid forms, but by means of line it is possible to convey artfully an idea of areas and contours, thus giving an abstract rendering of an object sufficient for many purposes. To the constructor it is indispensable, and for illustrations it serves perfectly.

The primary forms of art, as evidenced by the incised bones of animals of prehistoric times, and the child caricatures of to day, are lines only,

46

Plate VIII.

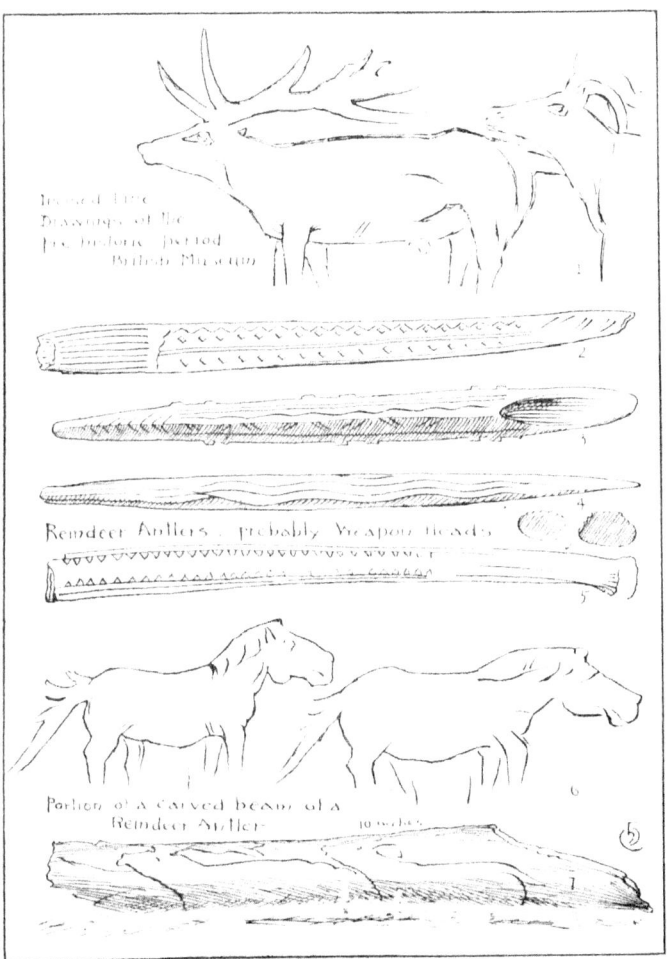

OUTLINE DRAWINGS, PRE-HISTORIC. BRITISH MUSEUM.

Plate IX.

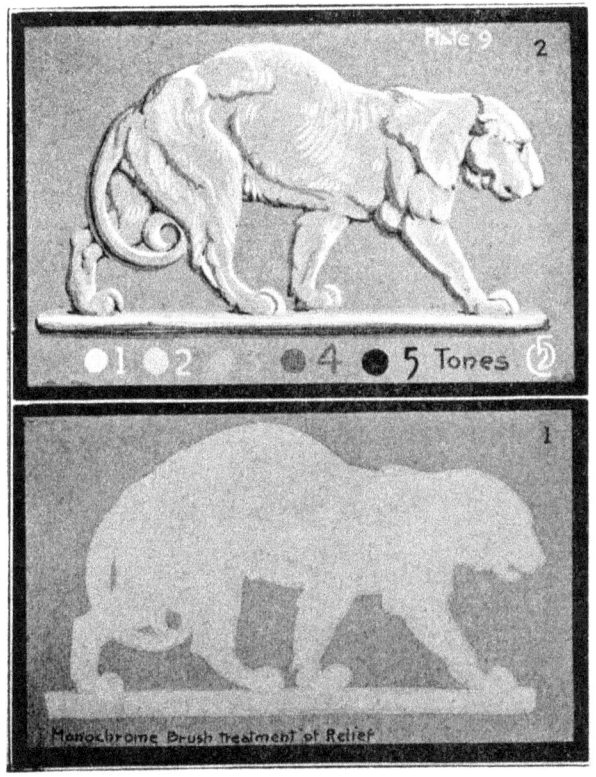

TONE STUDY PAINTED IN MONOCHROME FROM THE CAST.

Plate X.

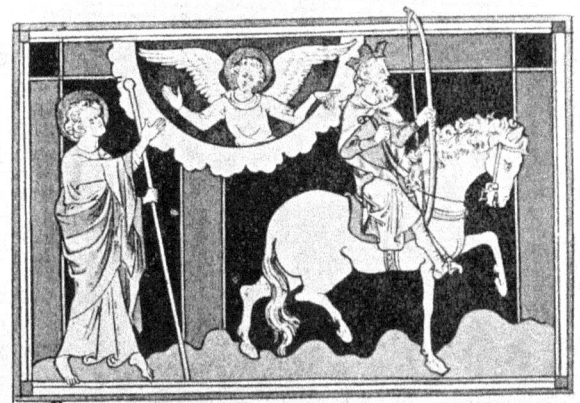

Seo vi les signeus our ouert vn des sertis · ec oe se auare testes me vir · siu
st coine voz de rouepte · veues veer · Or ico vi vn blanc cheual istr· a al
oi · eir eure · our arx · ec ccone sui est sone .

su le cheual blanc est signesie seire, ec il issie en vencaut pur vencre eglise
gest nette de pentsie par baptesme · pur la mort issu crist · Ciel oi seer—
—uare signiste le siz dieu par se ark · c'est signiste saut escripture ge mandre les
maufesauiz par le iugemeutz par la ccoune ge sui est sone, signiste le teeple
de paens ge ec est couerrez a sui Coo gil issi en veueaut pur veutre, signiste
ge il couertra les crose par geuye gil euuerra vers la sou del mounde

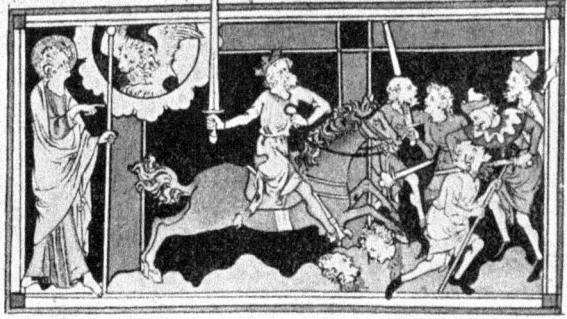

leaving to the imagination of the spectator the completion of the picture, in colour, light, shade, etc. (Plate VIII., figs. 1 to 7).

From this line treatment, proceed to colour, blot, or sunk ground (Plate IX., figs. 1 and 2), and we are nearer a realisation, by contrast of tones of dark and light. The "flat" relief of Greek sculpture, the colour masses of Greek pottery or Mediæval inlaid tiles, give areas of various sized masses, effective at a distance and decoratively valuable, yet still far from the reality. Silhouette or shadow figures are examples generally satisfying as far as they go.

By the addition of flat colours, a nearer approach is made to Nature, local colour being given, as a red rose with green leaves, a flesh-coloured face with coloured costume. The areas thus broken produce secondary silhouettes, which may be marred, if not carefully balanced in tone and tint. Appliqué embroidery of different stuffs, flat cotton printing, weaving, mosaic, etc., are examples of this class of treatment. Then outlined forms, with colours filled in, the outline defining and detailing, and suggesting textures, as in Japanese block printing, poster printing, pottery painting of the Persian and the Italian Renaissance, and Mediæval manuscripts (Plate X.), Cloisonné enamel, carpet weaving, etc., where the line prevents the colours from impinging and becoming muddy. Such strong lining is of great value in stained glass, in which the uniting leads demand also the fullest structural consideration.

Another treatment, in which the outline is *omitted*, depends on contrasts of light and shade as well as colour, to distinguish one form from another, and accidents of growth and movement, are introduced in such a way as to give the most real effect. Picture and scene painting furnish examples, also lithographic and other modern mechanical printing processes have obtained great accuracy. Imitative realism of this kind is seldom decorative, as it generally claims undue attention for itself, to the detriment of the whole scheme.

Preliminary Exercises with the Brush.

The brush is the readiest means of expressing forms on a plane surface.

Plate XI., figs. 1 to 4, give examples of typical primary forms easily rendered with the brush. Such forms are of constant occurrence in nature, singly or combined, the tapering one occurring in almost every form of life, from vegetable to human, and the relative length and width of these forms in varied proportions, giving, when curved, suggestions of activity and movement (Plate XI., figs. 9 to 12).

We have already noticed the variety of brushes, and that special shapes will give certain effects better than others. Thus, for " blot " work they should be selected to give units, and these can be repeated in many ways, much after the manner

Plate XI.

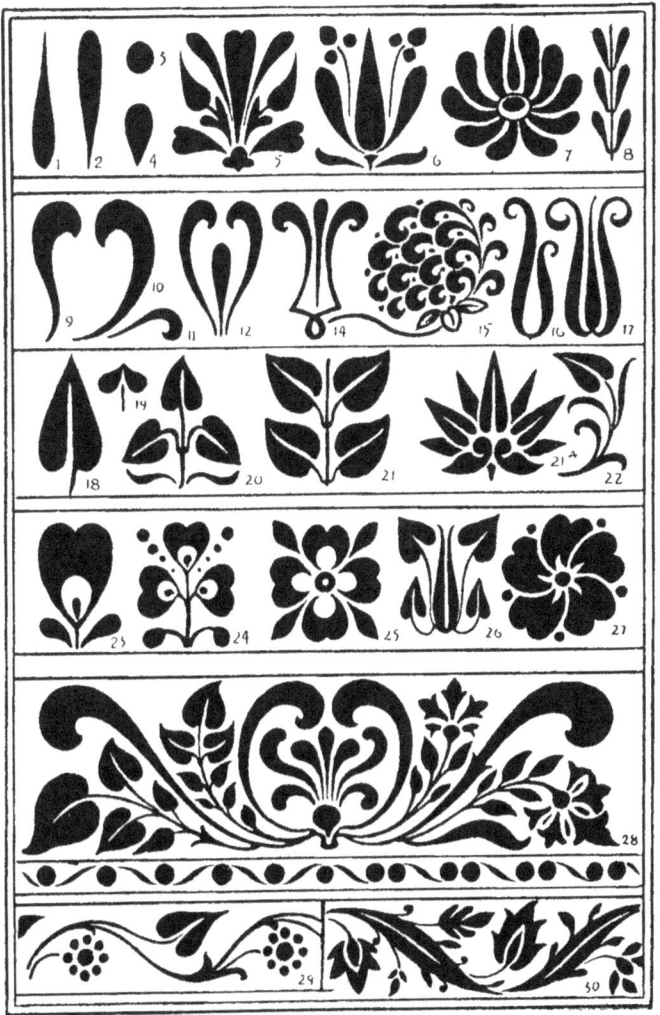

TYPICAL BRUSH-WORK FORMS.

Plate XII.

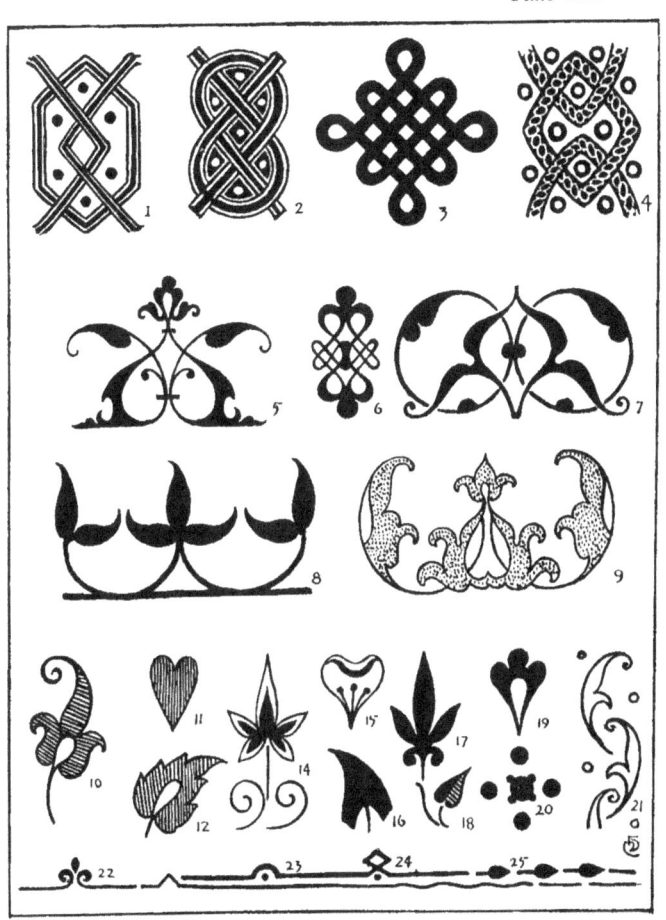

TYPICAL FORMS OF BOOKBINDERS' STAMPS.

of the bookbinder's ornament, which is produced
by means of stamps of simple leaf or petal shapes,
pressed on the leather. Grouped in twos and threes,
and combined with others they give great variety
(Plate XII., figs. 1 to 25). Effects arising from
simple pressure of the brush and colour are limited
in size and variety, and must necessarily be of a
mechanical nature. Decoratively useful, and forming good exercises in arrangement, this "blot"
work yet falls so far short of the possibilities of
brush treatment, as to be useful chiefly for the
amusement of juniors.

The examples of brush work given on Plate XI.,
figs. 5, 8, and 14 to 30, will be useful for practice,
and should be taken consecutively. Figs. 14 and
21A, for instance, repeated at regular distances,
between two lines, form a border; fig. 6 may be
used alternately with fig. 25, and so on. The plans
of arrangement for the designs on Plates XIV. and
XVII., form very good bases for original designs
for this purpose.

Ink, or stain, as described previously, will be the
best medium to use, and a goose-quill sable brush
with a good point. Practise drawing with the
point, and filling in the mass (see Plate II.). For
shapes about an inch long, draw the brush from
left to right, up and down, as the arrows indicate
(see diagram on page 60). The brush handle
should be nearly perpendicular to the paper,
and the stroke is to be taken, bending the

finger joints rather than moving the whole hand.
After practising this carefully, try similar shapes
about three inches long; this will compel movement
of the wrist, and perhaps the elbow, and so on,
exercising all the joints of the arm and hand.

Care must be taken to ensure accurate shapes
of the details, drawing with the point of the brush
and filling in the mass before the outline dries.
If the area of the pattern is too small, add to it;
endeavour though to have all right at first, and
not lightly guess at anything.

The details on Plate XIX., will afford endless
exercises, and Japanese picture books, books on
natural history and botany, and better than all,
Nature herself, will prove most delightful if studied
in this simple abstract way. Some further suggestions will be found at the end of the book.

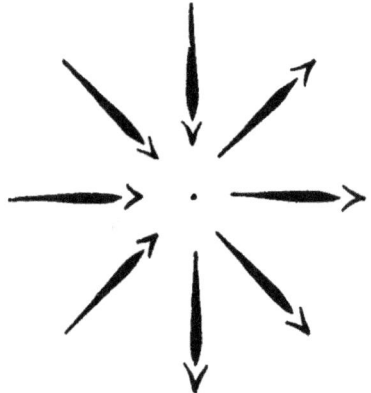

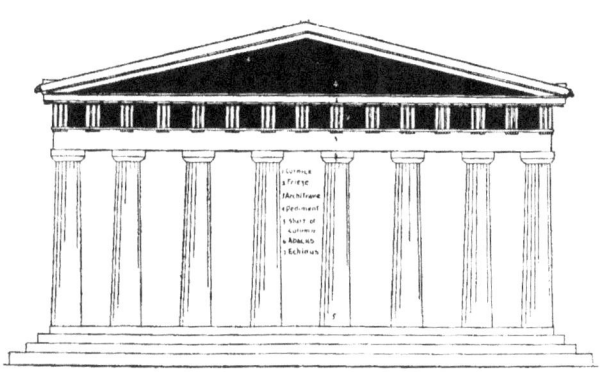

CHAPTER IV.

ELEMENTARY FORMS OF ORNAMENT.

THE SQUARE STYLE.

WHILST proceeding with the manipulation of
the brush as indicated in the previous chapter,
it will be well at this stage to notice some
of the influences which underlie the more important styles in ornament of former times, and
which are still in vogue, more or less modified
and adapted to present use.

An examination of the art work of the past
reveals the fact that construction has greatly influenced it, and that a few simple types have
prevailed, and have given a distinct character
peculiarly effective in certain styles. The rectangle, circle, triangle, and ellipse, afford the primary

forms, and one or other is adopted and used with a remarkable consistency.

The rectangle is seen in Greek achitecture, both in the plan and elevation of the building. The windows and doors of the beam and column type present severe and simple construction, remarkable in the proportions of the parts to the whole. The thickness and height of column, of entablature, and of the mouldings and their contours, are all carefully calculated for strength, combined with grace and beauty ; the ornamention is chaste and refined in itself, and in perfect harmony with the whole.

The Parthenon illustrated on page 61 gives an example of a marble structure, probably adapted from a wooden one, as there are corresponding structural parts which are used decoratively.

The entablature is divided into three bands as indicated, and the frieze is generally the band which receives the most important decoration. In some examples it is divided into panels, and the severe contrast of horizontal and vertical lines gives an expression of stability and repose. In other examples the frieze is continuous, and is decorated with repeating patterns of the honeysuckle, or with processions of figures.

In this early Greek period the slanting line seldom occurs, except in the roof. Inclined lines and masses suggest movement and activity. These occur chiefly in the ornament on the non-structural parts, and the spaces, such as panels in the frieze and tympanum. Intermediate stages of inclination, from vertical to horizontal, suggest a state of unrest, but two opposed falling lines arrest and support each other, giving repose such as is seen in Gothic architecture, where oblique lines play an important part.

This subject is treated very succinctly in " Line and Form," by Walter Crane.

In Elizabethan architecture the treatment of wood panelling is generally rectangular and has a restful effect. Economy of construction is an important factor, as wood panelling is most easily made if rectangular, and the stronger frame leads to the use of thinner panels.

The joiner, as the name indicates, makes larger panels than could be otherwise obtained from a single board, the simplest method being to place strips of wood side by side, and to fix battens across at right angles (Plate XIII., fig. 22), or, to clamp the ends as in a drawing board.

The framed construction (Plate XIII., fig. 23) commonly used, gives opportunities for varied proportions of styles, frames, and panels, so that from the simple cabinet door to the old wainscotted rooms, or the Italian choirstalls, beauty of construction and proportion are carefully expressed. Ceilings of the Renaissance period are often divided by beams necessary to support the floor above, thus forming convenient spaces for boarding over, and giving recesses or coffers. When moulded and decorated these ceilings form beautiful examples, in which construction controls the decorative treatment.

Flat.   Fillet · Tenia

Students cannot make too many notes and measurements of the proportions of old panelled walls and ceilings ; they not only serve to train the eye to a proper appreciation of cause and effect, but also as excellent bases for adapting to the division of other surfaces and even for translation and use in other classes of work, such as painting, bookbinding, etc.

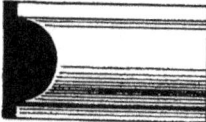

Convex.   Torus.

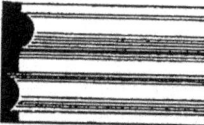

Convex.   Bead.

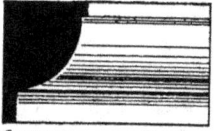

Convex.   Ovolo.
Echinus.

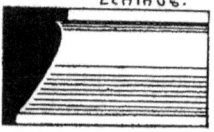

Whilst on this subject, we may briefly notice mouldings, which play such an important part in the beautifying of constructed forms. If we consider them as the ornamented edges of the framing, or as planted in the angle formed by two intersecting planes, or as the frame itself mitred at the corners, it will be seen they not only serve to modify abrupt angles, but that through their undulating surfaces, the broad and narrow lines of light and shade give a pleasant transition from one plane to another. They also serve to emphasise a change of contour, as in the capital of a Gothic pier, and on metal or other vase forms. By such simple means the architect refines his design and produces charming effects, and the carpenter renders his products more serviceable, as the acute angles of his wood-work are easily splintered. So the beams of the ceiling, the furniture, etc., have rounded or bevelled edges, which give a pretty play of light and shade.

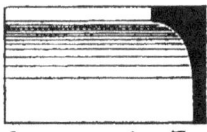

Concave. Cavetto

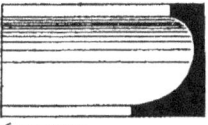

Concave.

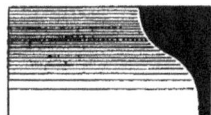

Compound. Cyma.

Ogee.

It is possible to obtain valuable hints from groups of mouldings for the arrange-ment of painted lines ; lines of dark and light colour, lines broad and narrow, the effect of which, if nicely proportioned, is very ornamental (Plate XIII., figs. 24, 25).

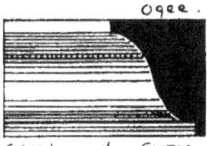

Compound. Cyma.

Cyma reversa.

Generally in old work the craftsman has been careful to place round and hollow and

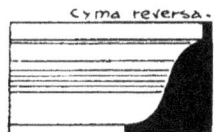

flat sections in such order and proportion as to contrast and give value to each other. Usually a hollow moulding succeeds a round or a flat one. It is seldom that two of the same section, or two of the same width and projection are placed together, and so the architect and craftsman play with light and shade and reflection effectively. This subject is, however, so extensive, that to test it fully would require a whole volume alone. For our purpose it must be sufficient to grasp the importance of making studies of groups of mouldings, particularly of their sections, and of the resultant effects of light and shade.

The diagrams given on pages 64 and 65 show sections of the four kinds of mouldings used in the classic styles—*i.e.*, flat, round or convex, hollow or concave, and compound or concavo-convex. In Greek buildings the sections were usually of flattened curves, something like the egg. Similar mouldings were used in Roman buildings, but the sections were nearly arcs of circles ; and in the Italian Renaissance work of the sixteenth century the same mouldings were used, but refined in their curves and proportioned very beautifully.

It is interesting to notice that the decoration of each moulding is usually based on its own section, thus developing the contour instead of destroying it.

In Gothic buildings the mouldings show the introduction of inclined planes and of deep under-cutting, giving stronger contrasts of light and shade, so that chamfers, quirks, etc., are peculiar

Plate XIII

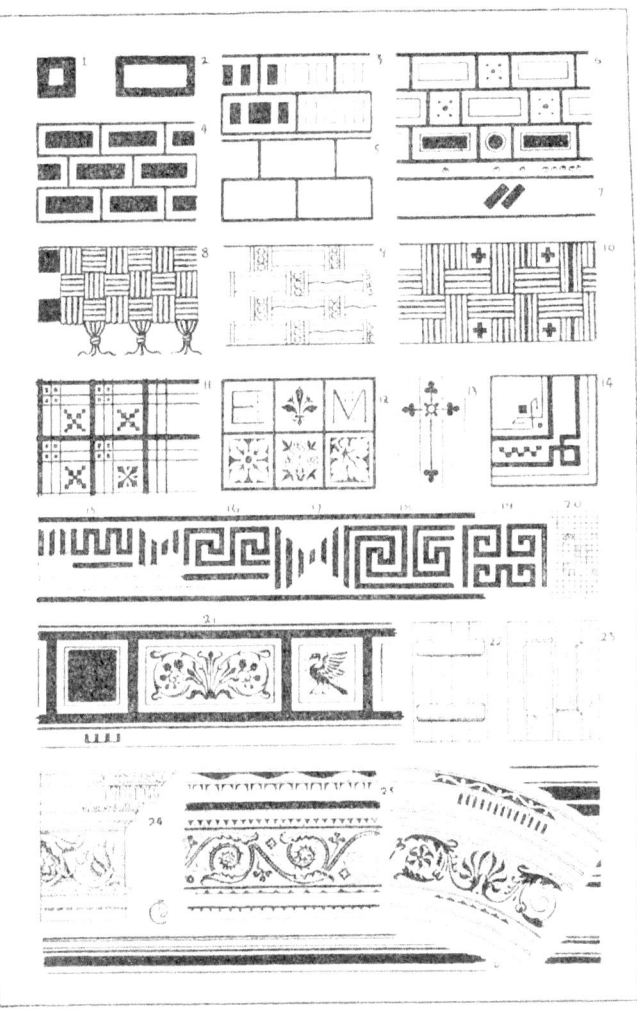

RECTANGULAR FORMS: STONEWORK, WEAVING, MATTING, ETC.

to certain periods of Gothic work (Plate XVI.,
figs. 1 to 4). The rectangle is of frequent
occurrence as a geometrical basis for repeating
patterns, and constructive arrangements of brick or
stone in one plane are capable of great variation.
Tiles, stamped bricks, and stencilled church decoration afford good examples (Plate XIII., figs.
1 to 7). Interlacing threads in weaving also give
endless variations, and a large class of fabrics
are patterned by these simple constructive forms,
the threads crossing at right angles, producing
effects by reflecting the light in varying degrees.
Basket work and matting show this perfectly. By
varying the colour and the quantity of threads
there is no limit to the patterns, as in stripes and
checks—*i.e.*, where coloured stripes are crossed,
or checked, at right angles with other colours,
producing mixtures of the two colours at the
crossing. Checks and plaids are the simplest and
most primitive ornaments, and form the greater
part of textile patterns.

Plate XIII., figs. 10 and 11, shows variations
of weaves, with the introduction of simple floral
forms, which give the beginning of many pretty
combinations.

Greek frets or keys are rectangular, and are
often used in decoration ; the bars of the key are
usually about the same width as the spaces between, so giving an even quantity valuable in
textiles. Plate XIII., fig. 15, is a single key ;

fig. 16, is an L key, and so on, and the most elaborate arrangements of running keys can be made by designing on the square plan indicated in fig. 20. Bi-symmetrical keys, in which the ground gives a T shape, have their movements restrained by a turn-over (fig. 18). Fig. 19 is a broken key—*i.e.*, not continuous ; it is a treatment occurring in Chinese and Peruvian patterns.

Ornament of this kind is usually applied to flat surfaces, such as a frieze or floor border, and in mosaic or small tile work, where it is very effective, severe, and restful, but without any particular interest or association. In Eastern ornament similar forms are used, but the oblique line is introduced, the spacing is greatly varied, and elaborate interlacings give greater complexity.

Straight lines and lines at right angles are not of common occurrence in nature ; crystals, rocks, and perhaps a few stems of plants, are the nearest approach, and they are almost always modified by gentle curves or fractures.

Man's work is mechanically perfect in this respect, as in building, where the wood, stone, and iron are dressed quite perfectly ; but nature is ever disturbing the perfection. This is seen in engineering work and in old buildings, where settling and the action of the elements are constantly at work, modifying and varying, to the delight of the picture painter.

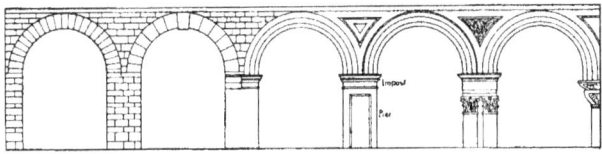

THE CIRCLE STYLE.

The adoption of the circular arch form of construction by the Romans, two thousand years ago,
was accompanied by a great change in the character
of the decoration.   In their colossal buildings
some other means of roofing than that afforded
by beams was necessitated.

The arch, used previously by the Assyrians, was
employed ; the ingenious arrangement of wedge-
shaped stones or bricks was so ordered towards
a centre, that the pressure from above tended to
make the whole stronger.   Thus, a dome of 140-ft.
span was constructed, and vaults, niches, and other
circular forms were devised, which give shapes,
both concave and convex, with spaces such as
spandrils, etc., between, for the consideration of
the decorator—features inseparable from Roman,
Romanesque, and Renaissance architecture.   Co-
incident with these, scrolls, volutes, and geometric
arrangements of circles and squares were freely
used, and were quite in harmony with the whole.

The circle, in combination with the straight line,

gives a playful character, the curve suggesting movement.

In the window openings, doorways, and panellings, the arch shape is frequently employed, just as in such parts in the Greek style the rectangle prevailed. A consistency common in most developed styles is noticeable, and since the lesser forms are of the same character as the greater, so furniture, metal work, etc., partook of this curved influence.

The diagram on page 71 shows a simple arrangement of bricks in arch form, resting on piers or rectangular supports of great thickness, in order to bear the thrust or pressure outwards. The head of the pier on which the arch rests is called the impost, and is usually emphasised by a group of mouldings, as on Plate XV., fig. 28. Panels are sunk on the faces of the pier, which give a lighter appearance, and these have received the devoted attention of some of the greatest decorators. Sculptured or painted arabesques, generally so delicately treated as to preserve the supporting effect of the pier, form a peculiar feature of this style.

Plate XV., fig. 1, shows the arch faced with stone, suggesting a bent architrave, the appearance of "springiness" and strength being enhanced by the bands, or fasciæ. This feature is seldom decorated, its beauty depending on the simple curved lines and planes receiving the light.

The Greek beam and column construction was

used in this style also, and was often applied as a facing to an arched building, one order being sometimes placed over another. Where the whole round column gave too much projection, half-round columns were used, or flat pillars of slight projection, useful perhaps as buttresses, whilst giving good decorative effect.

At a later period the pier was treated as a pillar, with a capital and base, and a small portion of the entablature, giving the idea of a second capital supporting the arch. So we have here the beginning of innumerable variations—arches interlacing, producing the pointed form (Plate XV., fig. 14) ; clusters of pillars, and such forms as occur in the Romanesque style, and down to Norman times (Plate XV., fig. 2). Then in this country these are superseded by the pointed Gothic arch (Plate XV., fig. 6) and the oblique line influence ; and ultimately the frieze and pilaster which find but little patronage until the revival or Renaissance in Europe in the fifteenth century.

In Nature a perfect sphere or circle is seldom seen, but the form is the constructive basis of many objects ; for instance, in such flowers as the buttercup, rose, and apple, we have a centripetal construction, in which the petals form cup shapes (Plate XIV., fig. 1). In the higher organic forms, there is almost an absence of mechanical curves, such as the compass describes so easily. The iris of the eye is perhaps the exception in the human figure, and in most animal forms curves of a varied degree are usually seen in the healthy creature. Overfeeding may distend, and produce an ugly plumpness, as may be seen in the overfed pet collie, which lacks the beauty of the active shepherd's dog.

The opposite is seen in the angular character, brought about by starvation and fatigue, or by overwork, whether mental or physical, and in any case such extremes of the normal condition seldom afford types of the beautiful, although often an approach to either stage has much charm of character, as the babe with its chubby cushions of fat, or the old warrior with his wrinkles and battle scars.

In drawing, the natural tendency of the hand is to form curves. The arm, from the shoulder, can be used for large circles, if the elbow and wrist are kept still, and from the elbow and the wrist smaller circles are easily described, whilst the finger-joints give small curves. The earlier these joints are exercised, the greater the ease with which facility will be acquired. All this is included in the term Freehand, and in this, as in all freedom, the more the contributing parts are under control, the greater the power.

It is said that Giotto, a great Italian artist of the thirteenth century, was " asked by the Pope's envoy to submit a drawing, in proof of his talent and ability to execute certain work. Giotto took an ordinary brush full of colour, and, steadying his arm, described a perfect circle on an upright panel with a sweep of his wrist, thus showing the importance the artist attached to precision of workmanship."

Ruskin recommends the student to draw circles freehand—to train him to habits of precision. " It is one of the most difficult forms ; it appears to be so, because any one can see an error in a circle."

Plate XIV. gives arrangements of ornament based on circular plans. Fig. 1 is a group of leaves or sepals and petals, common to many flowers. The sepals (dark) fit over the joining of the edges of the petals. Each kind of flower has its special number of divisions ; for instance, roses and buttercups have five. Fig. 2 gives examples of such arrangements as we see in the daisy, dandelion, and other lowly growing plants, suggesting very appropriate decorative treatment for horizontal surfaces, such as floors and ceilings. The kaleidoscope, with its three mirrors, shows the value of this repeating round a centre, for by its means irregular bits of glass, pins, or threads, etc., yield pretty effects. These multi-symmetrical patterns are useful in mosaic tile work, and as foundations for numerous geometric repeats.

Figs. 4 and 5, Plate XIV., are patterns formed on a " turn-over," or bi-symmetrical plan. As mentioned previously, a piece of mirror, unframed, placed on its edge to reflect an object, or part of one, will show the decorative value of this arrangement, which is frequently used for woven fabrics—one-half only being designed, and the "turn-over" automatically effected in the loom.

Fig. 5, Plate XIV., has the centre of radiation within the circle, and it is emphasised by a dark mass (the calyx), and the florets are all curved to flow harmoniously into the outer circle, whilst fig. 4 has the centre of radiation some distance below—a common plan in many natural forms, such as plants springing from the ground, as rhubarb and celery, or feathers in the wing and tail of a bird, or the fingers of the hand—the hidden centre giving more mystery and beauty.

These arrangements may, of course, occur in other shapes besides the circle, and are great factors in preventing monotony. In the case of long parallel lines of buildings, they invariably appear to radiate from a distant centre, as illustrated by the principles of perspective.

Figs. 6-23 give bands of ornament based on the circle, some interlacing like twining ropes, others like the links of a chain, and others again like arches, or festoons ; these latter remind us that actual plants used on festival occasions may have given rise to such forms, and our modern harvest and Christmas decorations give further suggestions for similar treatment. By the way, much of the best ornament has been inspired by realities, modified or developed so as to produce

Plate XIV.

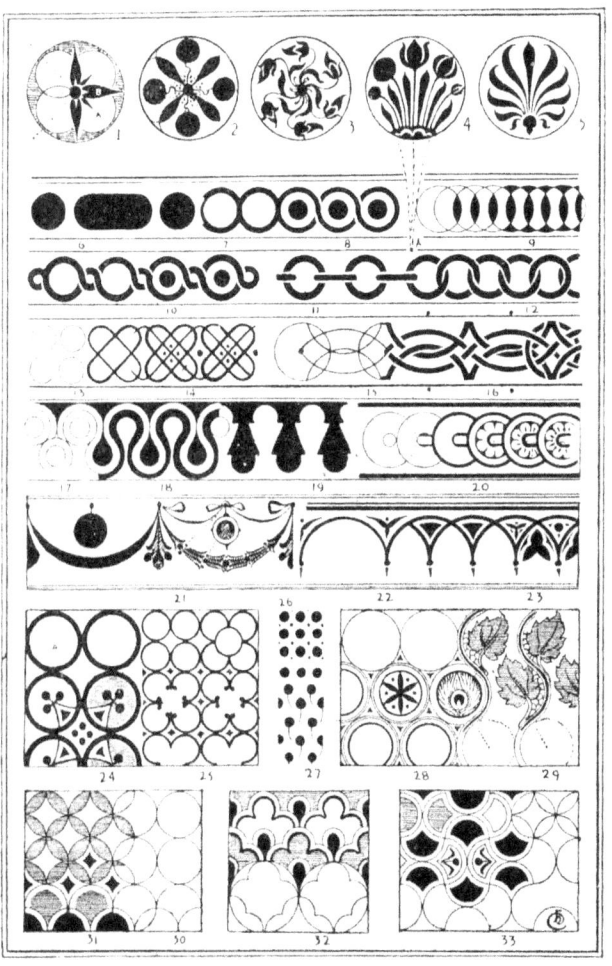

DECORATIVE FORMS EVOLVED FROM THE CIRCLE.

a good effect. We noticed the ceiling decorations arising from beams in construction. Another kind of ceiling decoration may have been suggested by an awning suspended overhead, giving fan shapes in the corners. Many Italian ceilings are decorated on this plan (Plate XV., fig. 12).

Plate XIV., figs. 22, 23, gives examples of arched patterns used effectively on Greek pottery, the curves being beautifully varied on their convex surfaces. Similar arrangements with the arches "cusped," as in Plate XIV., fig. 23, are characteristic of the Gothic style.

Figs. 24-33 give types of bases useful for repeating patterns, for wall-papers, carpets, etc., all evolved from the circle, and capable of infinite variations. Plate XV., figs. 17-21, shows the ogee, with varied treatments: in some the stem, in others the leaf or flower centre, is most forcible.

It will be seen from the foregoing that the most elaborate repeats can be reduced to some few simple construction lines.

Of books on this subject, two by Lewis F. Day, "The Anatomy of Pattern" and "Planning of Ornament," will be found most useful.

Generally it is best to work on some geometrical plan, otherwise objectionable features may present themselves in the final effect.

Plate XV., figs. 13-16, shows different treatments of ornament, chiefly influenced by the architectural shapes; figs. 14 and 15 giving patterns for friezes or dadoes based on arcadings, as in Byzantine work. Fig. 1, Plate XV., is a pier, with arch and spandril of Italian character, derived from the ancient Roman style. The pilaster (fig. 29), decorated as briefly mentioned before, has been treated in various ways. Besides painting and sculpture, inlaid marble, or mosaic glass of the richest colours were applied, especially in the Pompeiian style (see also an adaptation of this to the border of a manuscript, Plate XXXIV).

Fig. 2, Plate XV., is a sketch of a doorway at Lincoln minster. The columns are arranged to step back successively, so that the arches recede inwards—a characteristic of Norman buildings; and instead of piers with pilasters, there are slender columns, each having a cap and base, and these are clustered together, giving a beautiful supporting effect. The shafts are often carved with low-relief patterns of zigzag, diaper, or interlacing ornament, giving richness of texture without interfering with their structural character.

Figs. 22-25 show discs and paterae used in Greek decoration. The petals are similar in size and shape, and were probably suggested by the centripetal arrangements in flowers, or by the beaten metal braziers used in ancient ceremonies.

Plate XV.

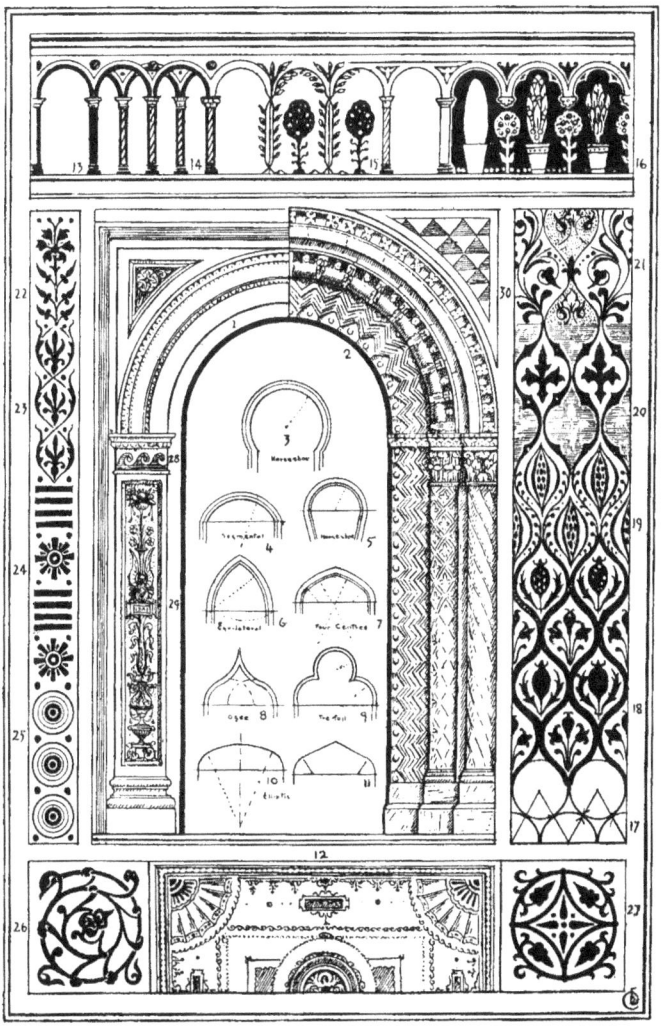

CIRCULAR ARCH CONSTRUCTION AND PATTERN.

THE POINTED STYLE.

The term " Pointed " is applied to the Gothic
style of architecture, chiefly because pointed arches
and gables are employed, the beam and the round
arch being set aside, and arches formed of pene-
trating arcs taking their places. There has been
much controversy as to its origin, some ascribing it
to the interlacing of circular arches, others to the
necessities of climate ; the high-pitched roof being
best for passing off heavy rains and snow. According to some, it was introduced by the Crusaders
from the East, and discoveries in Assyria show at
least the pointed arch, if not the gable, in use in
ancient times. However, for our purpose it is
sufficient to note that in the eleventh and twelfth
centuries the round arch, so long used in France
and England, was supplanted by the pointed form,
and not only were the elevation and plan altered
in shape to harmonise with it, but also the windows,
doors, panels, mouldings, and the·ornamental forms
which are used as decoration by the acute-angled
arch were all influenced.

We have already noticed that in any definite
style the greater affects the lesser. and all parts
become modified and rendered in perfect harmony ;
so in this style we see that the mouldings and
geometric decorations, with their sharp angles and
curves, are in keeping with the plan and elevation
of the building, and that inclined lines and planes

form prominent features. In the sculpture deep undercutting gives to the details strongly contrasting shadows, effective in the western climate. Thus the artist works upon natural principles, for in Nature there is the persistence of certain typical forms with but slight variations. And as in trees the small twigs are similar to the larger in structure and shape ; so in the human figure, as in those of quadrupeds, birds, etc., tapering forms are seen, the leg, arm, fingers, being similar in shape, whilst in groups of foliage, mountain contours, clouds, etc., the characteristics of the lesser divisions are of a similar quality to the larger groups, usually of a radiating tendency from different centres. Thus unity of effect is ensured, and the whole affords excellent suggestions for the designer.

Tapering forms, as already pointed out, are prevalent in Nature. Parallel lines are seldom

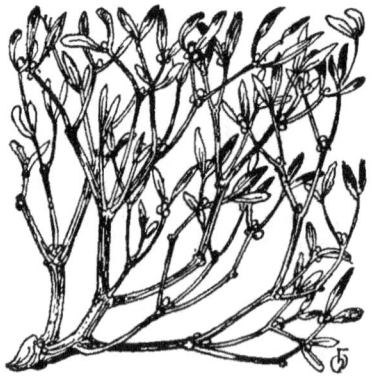

seen, and so we have beautiful gradations of light and shade, of quantities and colour, seldom without unity and harmony.

In the stems of plants some uniform angle will be observed in the

Plate XVI.

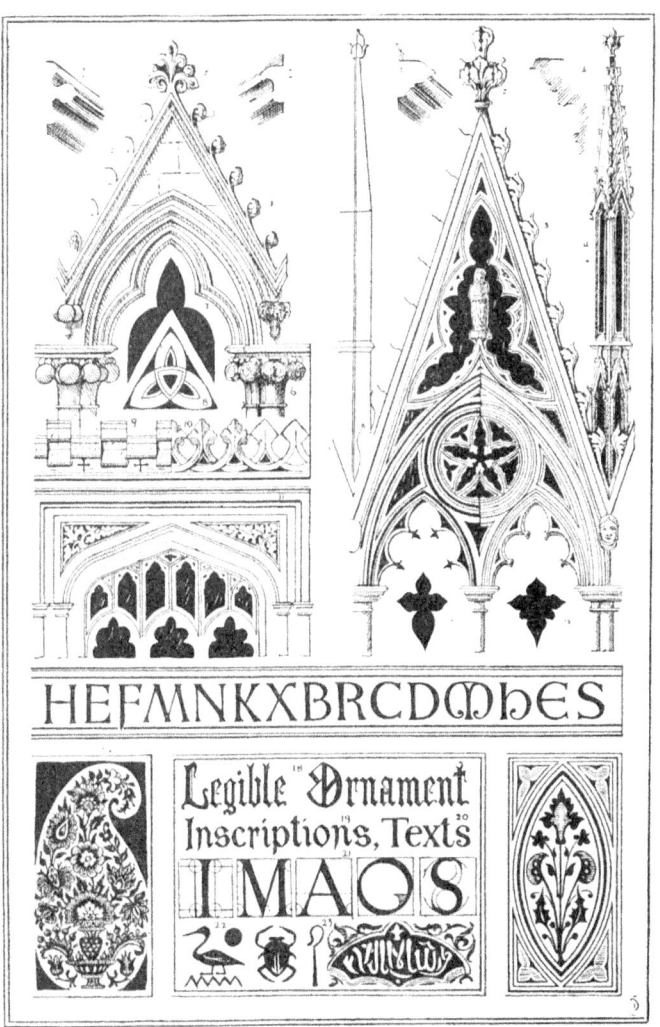

FORMS CONSTRUCTED ON A TRIANGULAR BASIS.

junctions of the branches, the character belong-
ing to each species greatly depending on this
peculiarity. A branch of mistletoe shows this in
an extreme degree (see illustration on page 84).
The poplar tree has branches almost vertical, whilst

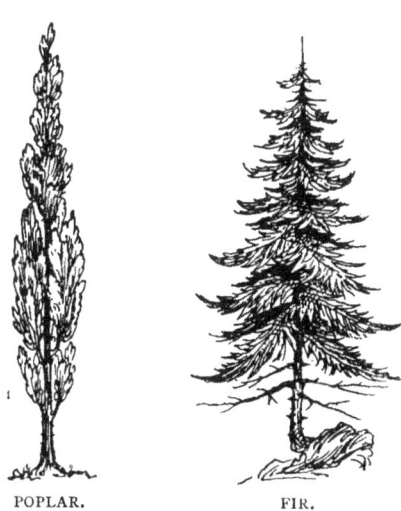

POPLAR.   FIR.

the fir or larch have them horizontal, and between
these two extremes there are innumerable variations.

The degree of inclination which lines and surfaces
have to each other is very important, and should
be carefully rendered even though such lines may
be only short, as (say) the nose in relation to the
forehead and other features, which, if not treated
quite accurately in this respect, will alter the

whole expression of the face. As a pyramidal form fixed on the face it is varied in its proportion and inclination in different individuals very remarkably. And in the gables and arches of the different periods of Gothic architecture, the sharpness or flatness of the arch and its curves gives distinctive character to each of the three divisions of the style.

We have seen examples of forms based on simple curves struck from one centre. In the pointed style two or more centres are used, and the arcs penetrate each other more or less acutely. Figs. 3 to 11, Plate XV., give examples, with centrings in some instances outside the arch. Keeping the centres on the line of spring, ensures a pleasant flow of the curve into the straight line of support. An abrupt junction is obtained if the centres are above or below the spring line of the arch (figs. 3 and 4).

In the earliest period of Gothic (the Early English), the arch is equilateral and is used with acute-angled gables and mouldings (Plate XVI., figs. 1 and 6), buttresses, and pinnacles ; while in the plans of buildings, the hexagon and octagon are used. Shafts, with cap and base, are clustered round a central pier, and the foliated ornament is generally of a trefoil type (Plate XVII., fig. 18).

In the second, or " Decorated," period similar forms, but more elaborated, were generally used. Plate XVI., figs. 12 and 16, from Winchester, illustrate the use of geometric shapes in the gables and window heads. In some examples this tracery rather resembles the branches of trees, notably in Lincoln minster. Windows are arranged in groups. Canopies or ornamental gables, forming niches (Plate XVI., fig. 12), are of common occurrence. The arches are often "cusped" and of double curves, "ogee," and the mouldings partake of the same elaborate treatment, whilst the floral decorations are derived from Nature, and afford the most beautiful examples of ornamental treatment of local flora. The ivy, vine, oak, maple etc., give great interest ; though in some examples naturalism is indulged in to the sacrifice of decorative effect.

The third, or "Perpendicular" style has, as the name implies, many lines perpendicular to each other in the window tracery (Plate XVI., fig. 11), wall panelling, etc. Further, the arch is generally flattened, and the roof is almost horizontal ; battlements (Plate XVI., fig. 9) form an important finish to the wall, and call to mind their use in castles and halls, for defence. Haddon Hall is a beautiful example, the ceilings and walls being decorated with geometric panels. Generally, the foliated ornament is very formal (Plates XVI., fig. 10, and XVII., fig. 17), and quite subservient to the structural shape, often fully filling the square or lozenge on which it is placed. The change from one style to another was gradual, and the transitional stages present very beautiful effects, with at times some strange mixtures of incongruous details. Thus, Italian Renaissance details are mixed with Gothic forms, and ancient mythical creatures with Christian symbols.

In Indian and Persian architecture and decoration, pointed arches and openings are used extensively, in wood, metal, stone, enamel, and painting ; whilst in textiles, woven or printed, cusped pointed panels and borders are used for changing ground colours. A curved form resembling a pine cone is used in the designs of Eastern carpets and Cashmere shawls (Plate XVI., fig. 24) which imparts to them a well-marked character. Shapes resembling leaves are used for grouping the smaller details together, and in Eastern art give rise to "inhabited" patterns, which are usually accompanied with a change of ground colour.

In Christian art certain geometric forms are used as symbols (Plate XVI., fig. 25). The vesica, a fish-shape, the trefoil (fig. 8), and interlacing circles and triangles symbolise the Trinity, Eternity, etc. Such signs were used by the early Christians to express certain ideas, and they are still employed in church decorations for their meaning and associations.

The letters of the alphabet are interesting in this respect, as symbols of sounds or of ideas. Originally simple renderings of natural forms, they are now clever combinations of the square, circle,

Plate XVII.

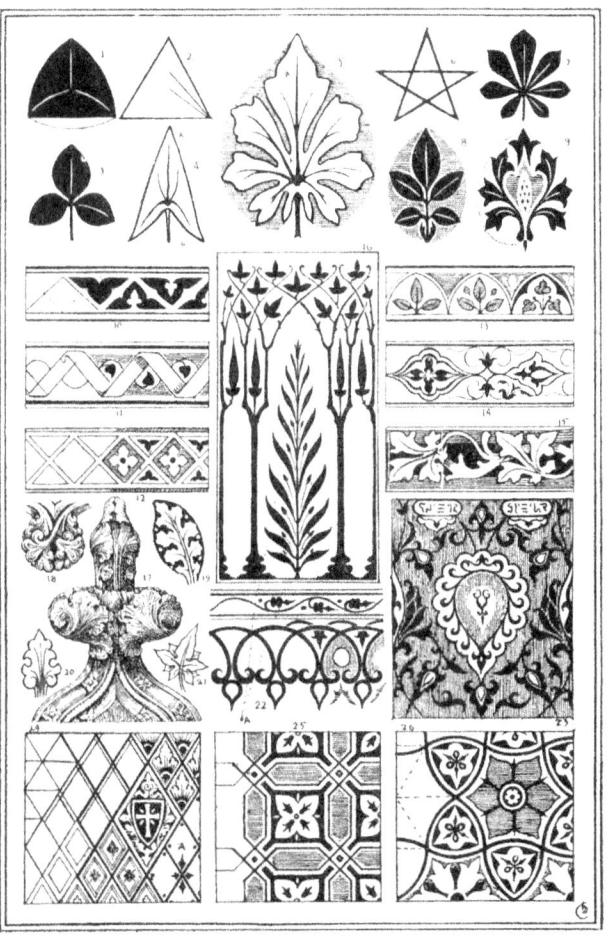

BORDERS, DIAPERS, ETC., ON A TRIANGULAR BASIS.

and triangle, being in the best work properly proportioned and spaced, and giving beautiful decorative effects.

The thin upstroke and thick downstroke are usually as in pen-writing. In the Roman and Italian types the letters in their graceful simplicity are so many decorative units, and words formed with them present varied arrangements of curved and straight lines, contrasting beautifully, apart from the meaning they convey.

Lettering, used for borders ; round the arches of a church ; or on a frieze or string course, gives a decoration of great value, in careful hands.

Mnemonic (aid to memory) is a term applied to lettering used in this way, and, in the Arabian style, texts from the Koran are freely used to give interest to their elaborate geometric ornament on textiles, pottery, etc., in the absence of forms derived from Nature, which were excluded by the restrictions of their creed (Plates XVI., fig. 23, and XVII., fig. 23).

Egyptian hieroglyphics, on the other hand, are directly derived from Nature (Plates XVI., fig. 16, and XIX., fig. 22), and include the owl, beetle, hawk, ibis, and many plant forms ; but they are always treated very simply, as symbols of the creatures rather than imitations, and as expressions of sounds or ideas.

A careful study of the shaping and spacing of letters in early manuscripts and printed books will

well repay the designer. In the best work the
proportions are always beautiful, and the words
easily read. Usually the lettering is in keeping
with the architectural style. In Roman lettering
rectangular and circular forms prevail, whilst in
Gothic the pointed character is developed ; the
former suggest an origin in chisel-cut stone,
the latter in pen or brush strokes. In both
styles the letters are generally vertical, but when
inclined, the same angle is adhered to in every
letter—an important point, for otherwise the effect
is most irregular.

In type-printed letters each one occupies a square
or an oblong, for convenience in setting ; but in
hand-printed letters, the artist, whilst observing an
orderly arrangement, will introduce little variations
of shapes, and occasional overlapping, which, if not
carried so far as to confuse, may give a beautiful
effect, and express individual taste and feeling.

Figs. 20 and 21, Plate XVI., give Roman types ;
figs. 17 and 19, are Gothic. Plate XXXVIII.
gives further examples.

The diapers and borders given in Plate XVII.
are influenced by the oblique line, and afford good
examples of the effect arising from this feature.
Gothic and Eastern borders are generally on such
bases. Compare these with the circular effects.

CHAPTER V.

NATURAL FORMS.

THE three forms we have noticed might be called
mechanical, as they are easily produced by such
means. A fourth may be called the organic form,
as it is found in almost all living and moving objects,
and is composed of curves or contours of ever
varying proportion. The egg, ellipse, and volute
are of this nature.

By bending a tapering fishing rod, or whip, a
curve is produced which expresses activity and life
(Plate XVIII., fig. 1), and if the quickening of the
curve is continued, the spring-like shape of the
volute is obtained (fig. 4).

A weight suspended on the extremity of a young
tree branch causes it to bend in a similar way, and
in trees this weight is present in the foliage, though
it is more evenly distributed. In heavy fruit-
bearing trees this curvature is strongly emphasised,
and the effort of the branch to right itself, after
being relieved of its burden, is also evident in the

upward growth. The apple tree is a beautiful example of energy, every branch expressing the character of its life.

The curved lines of leaves and leaf stalks show great flexibility. Celery, rhubarb, and lettuce, are good illustrations of this quality. Fig. 5, on Plate XVIII., taken from a piece of Italian ornament, shows the value of such curves in decoration, and reminds one of the celery when cultivated.

Flowing water, the waves at the prow of a boat or breast of a swimming bird, also exhibit this characteristic, whilst in the movement of animals similar curvature is seen, as in the cat preparing to spring, fish in swimming, and in the human figure when its symmetry is disturbed by motion.

We have already noticed that curves of a mechanical kind are absent from the human figure, and from nature generally, yet here the greatest variety of line is found ; even the petals of flowers, the contour of fruits, seed-vessels, etc., show this. The parabola, hyperbola, and ellipse, give geometric examples of similar curves useful for mouldings and for the contour of vases. In the Greek and Renaissance styles, refined gradations of light and shade arise from sections of this kind, and their ornament owes much of its beauty to the delicate lines of growth suggested by such curves.

The volute (Plate XVIII., figs. 4 and 6) is seen in the unrolling of a fern frond, or of the forget-me-

Plate XVIII.

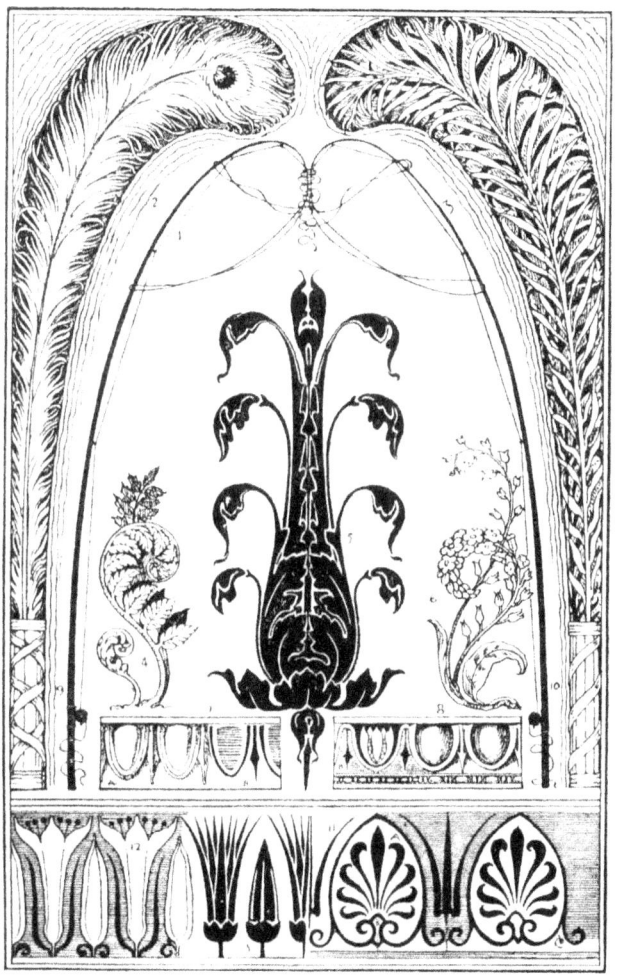

FLEXIBLE FORMS, OVALS, VOLUTES, ETC.

not ; and in shells, such as the periwinkle and snail, a spiral is seen somewhat like a thread wound on a cone (Plate XX., figs. 3 and 4), whilst in the tendrils of the passion flower, a spiral resembling the thread of a screw illustrates a common form seen in twining plants. A thread wound round a cylinder gives this form.

The volute lies in one plane and is an ornament characteristic of many styles. The New Zealander carves this form on his weapons, and tattoos it on his skin, and in Greek architecture curved forms like the ram's horn are used on capitals of columns, while the wave scroll, and scrolls ending in volutes are common in Roman and Italian ornament.

Greek vases afford beautiful examples of oval forms, which in many respects resemble seed-vessels. The rose berry (Plate XIX., fig. 5) poppy case, acorn (fig. 3), etc., are forms which may have suggested the shapes of bottles and other utensils. The gourd, when dried and the seeds extracted, is used for the conveyance of liquids, even at the present time in Spain and in the East, and imitations of it are of common occurrence in the pottery of those countries (Plate XXXII., fig. 3). Many other examples might be mentioned, but one more will suffice for our purpose: the cocoanut shell, which, used as a cup, sometimes mounted on a silver stand, answers its purpose admirably.

On Plate XIX. vase shapes are given. Figs.
6 and 12, are "amphoræ" used in Greece for
storing wines; the pointed end is pressed into
the earth, so that it stands upright and keeps
the contents cool. When used on a smaller scale
for other purposes it is placed in a ring tripod
stand.

The study of the ancient pottery of Greece
will well repay the designer, for not only are the
shapes beautiful, but their decorations are chaste
and perfectly arranged for effect.

We might continue with examples showing
the prevalence of these subtle curves in Nature
and in Art, finding in all the highest forms that
delicacy or vigour of curvature is ever present,
suggesting refinement and strength.

The human figure is considered as embodying
the perfection of these qualities, and the superior
character of Greek and Italian art is attributed to
a keen study of this subject. In the absence of the
entire figure for study, try to render the head,
hand, or foot, which are always available, and to
express the varied movements and changes, as
in the features, wherein the slightest variation
of line expresses a different character, and the
grouping of the fingers, etc., which are always
in harmony.

Nothing incites more to this than the use of the
brush, for in brush work the flexible tool, filled
with colour, pressed, drawn, or twisted on a surface,

gives varied beautiful shapes, as we have seen in Plates XI. and XII.

Plate XVIII., fig. 11, is the "Anthemion," one of a series of beautiful ornaments used by the Greeks in borders and bands. They are supposed to have been suggested by the flower of the honey-suckle. We can trace a similar arrangement of "florets" springing from a head, which in the painted treatment prevents confusion, and gives a good starting point for the radiation, and a mass contrasting with the lighter parts.

The thistle, chrysanthemum, and other compound flowers are grouped similarly to this. The florets resemble the stroke made by a flexible sable or camel-hair pencil, and in the decorations of vases they have by this means frequently been rendered in all periods. Greek vases give examples of the most beautiful kind of brush-work, the directness and freshness of the touches showing a complete mastery of the tool.

Running borders and diapers are produced by long and short brushes, each giving a different touch, and by grouping the touches in large and small quantities and on varied plans, they take the form of flowers and leaves, suggestive of different plants.

In Roman and Pompeiian art the acanthus leaf was produced by long brush strokes, arranged to radiate from certain points, which, when united by means of smaller strokes, gave the character of that plant. Fig. 14, Plate XIX., is a vine leaf with similar features, and one half is left incomplete, to show the effect of the brush strokes. By varying the tints of colour of such strokes, pretty gradated effects can be obtained, and effects having something of the beauty of relief work are given by using different tones of the same colour, as in monochrome painting. Figs. 1 and 2, Plate XXVII., are renderings from relief ornament in colour.

In Japanese decoration the brush is constantly employed, and such facility is acquired that their work affords most valuable lessons. Not only are vegetable forms rendered, but animals also, particularly birds, the suggestions of flight being perfect, See Plate XX., figs. 8, 11, and 12 ; Plate XXI., figs. 6 to 10 ; and Plate XXIII., fig. 11.

Plate XIX. gives many illustrations of forms naturally expressed by the brush. Fig. 8, gives curved forms, radiation in simple curves ; fig. 9, gives a compound curve ; fig. 13, a group with the thickest end of the strokes inwards ; figs. 1 and 5 are fruit and leaf forms ; figs. 10 and 11, centripetal flowers—all illustrating the prevalence of pointed and oval forms in Nature.

Again, figs. 16 to 22, Plate XIX., show some forms in animals, more or less elongated. The dolphin (Plate XIX., fig. 23) is a naturalistic treatment of this form, and fig. 24, is a conventional rendering, and depends much for its effect and

Plate XIX.

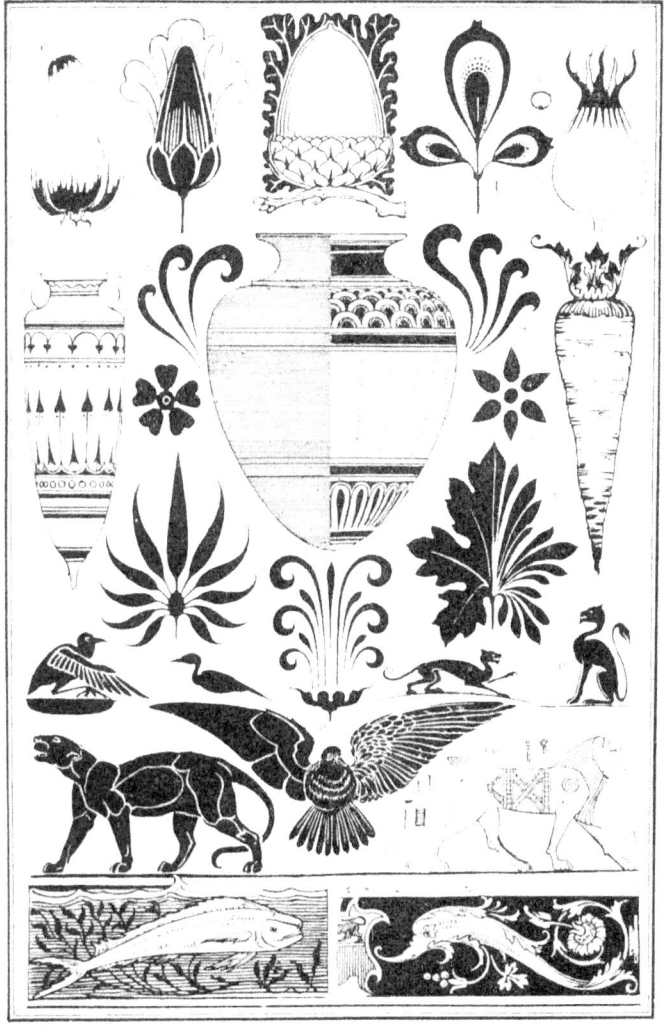

ORGANIC FORMS OF AN OVAL CHARACTER.

frequent use in Italian ornament, on its tapering, flexible form, enabling it to be bent and curved in harmony with other details ; the fins and tail are often foliated, and clothe the form somewhat after the manner shown. The tiger, fig. 21, is from a French sculpture, and is simplified in the style of Greek painted decoration, light outlines being left to define the chief divisions of the body and limbs. Fig. 22, a lion from a sculpture at Thebes, is a beautiful example of decorative adaptation. Fig. 20 shows a bird treated in silhouette and in detail ; and fig. 16 is an Egyptian rendering of a bird on its nest, wonderfully natural in its position.

Fig. 13, on Plate XVIII., is an Egyptian lotus and papyrus flower repeated, suggesting a probable basis of the Greek Anthemion.

The feather and palm, figs. 2 and 3, Plate XVIII., illustrate the springing character of a tapering stem, something like the fishing-rod on the same plate ; the leaves become further apart on the outside of the curve, and they overlap on the inside.

Fig. 7, on Plate XVIII., is a Greek egg-and-tongue moulding ornament. Fig. 8, is a similar moulding of the Roman period, showing a circular character ; A is a suggestion for adopting floral forms on the same lines for painted work, as in the Pompeiian style. Fig. 12, shows a lily arranged in the same way as the lotus and papyrus.

SHELLS AND FISHES.

Plate XX. illustrates a number of typical shells and fish forms—nature studies from various sources —the shells showing *radiation* and *spiral curvature*. The fish, figs. 8, and 11 are Japanese, and fig. 8 shows *imbrication* of scales beautifully, and treated as a stencil, the white portions being perforations, it is perfect as an illustration of ties forming part of the pattern. Fig. 11 is from a Japanese wood block print, the drawing for which is made on the wood with a brush and Indian ink. Fig. 12 is also a good example, and the value of the black mass is expressive of the dark purple shell of the creature in contrast with the lighter legs ; fig. 10 is from a book on Natural History, rendered into brush work, whilst fig. 9 is a direct copy of a woodcut in a similar book.

BIRDS.

Plate XXI. gives illustrations of decorative renderings of birds adapted to various materials. Fig. 1 is carved ivory, the bird curves harmonising with the circle. Fig. 4 is Greek vase painting and is full of brush character. Figs. 7 and 8 are also good examples of brush work on silk, by a Japanese artist. Figs. 6, 9, and 10 are examples

Plate XX.

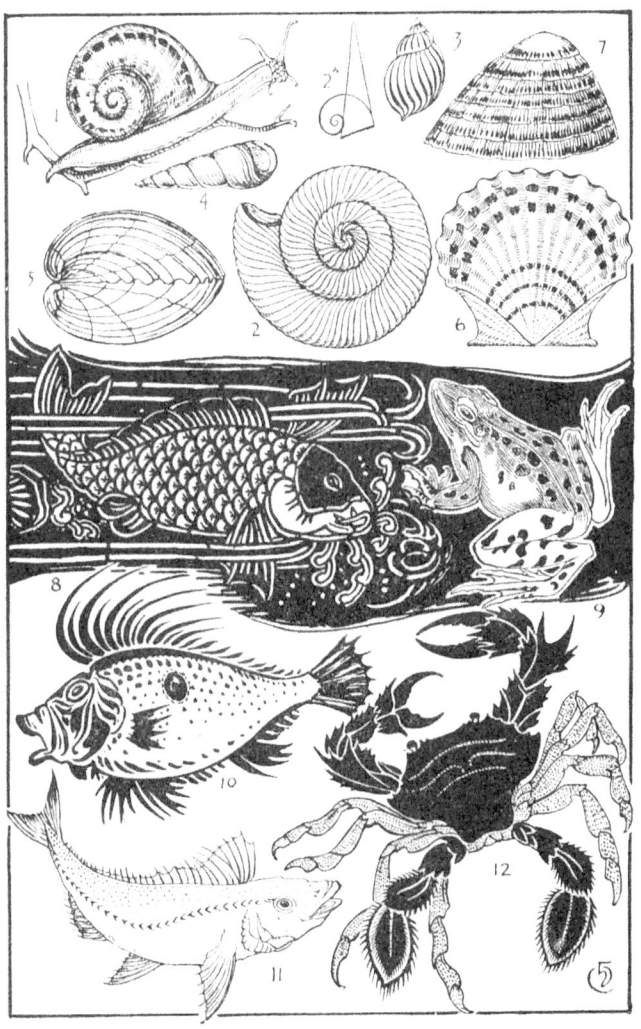

DECORATIVE TREATMENT OF SHELLS AND FISH.

Plate XXI.

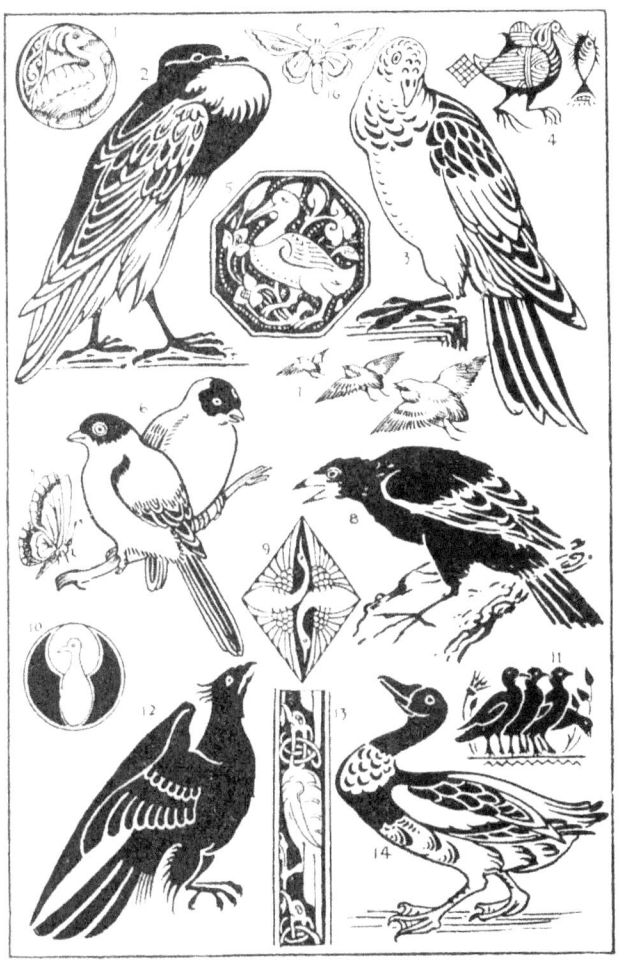

BIRDS TREATED FOR DECORATIVE WORK.

Plate XXII.

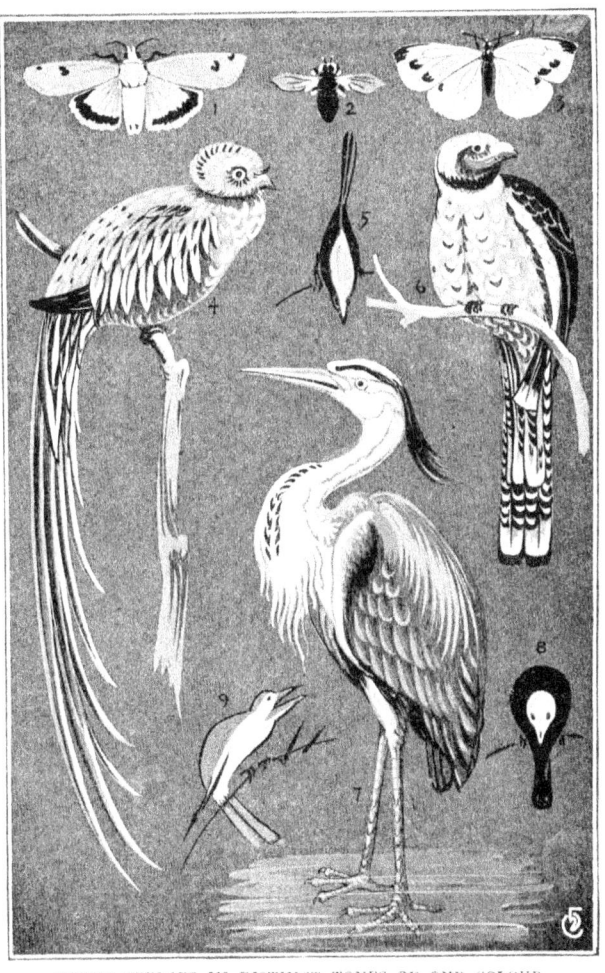

BRUSH STUDIES IN DISTINCT TONES OF ONE COLOUR.

of Japanese drawing, beautifully simplified ; fig. 10
reminding one of an inlay treatment. Fig. 5, a
Persian tile of gold lustre, shows a " saved " pattern—
i.e., one in which the background is painted out,
leaving the ornament in the original surface—a
sturdy little duck with floral forms, prettily spaced
and not interfering with the larger mass. Figs. 2,
3, and 14 illustrate the value of black masses to
express local tone. Fig. 12 is a flat silhouette
treatment of a bird on Sicilian silk of the twelfth
century, an excellent rendering for textile work,
the large masses of colour being broken by the
texture of the stuff. Fig. 11 is from an Egyptian
wall painting of birds by the riverside, the zigzag
line beneath representing water. Figs. 15 and
16 are from Nature. Fig. 13 is an extremely
conventional bird from a Celtic MS.

Plate XXII. is of birds, treated in tones in a
decorative way. Such renderings afford excellent
practice in brush work, using extremes of light
and dark on an intermediate toned silhouette, as
shown in Plate IX. The insects are copied from
nature and the birds from a Natural History,
and from stuffed specimens. Figs. 5, 8, 9 are the
simplest Japanese renderings of action.

QUADRUPEDS.

Plate XXIII. shows a variety of decorative treatments of quadrupeds for different purposes. Fig. 1 is from a Greek vase painting, black figure on red ground ; fig. 2 is from an Egyptian wall painting ; fig. 3 from a Celtic manuscript ; fig. 4 from an Early English Gothic tile ; figs. 5, 5 are examples of simple brush drawings of eyes, taken from Greek vases and given in Murray's " Guide to the British Museum." It is most interesting and instructive to notice how these conventionalities have set aside anything that would tend to confuse. Fig. 6 is a translation into brush work from the Elgin Marbles ; fig. 7 is from a Natural History ; fig. 8 is a Byzantine ivory carving, the ground being sunk and the raised pattern carved very simply ; fig. 9 is from a French Gothic sculpture, and is a good example of the grotesques and strange combinations peculiar to Gothic buildings ; fig. 10 is a German heraldic treatment of a lion, symbolising the chief characteristics of the creature and easily seen from a distance ; fig. 11 is from a Japanese book, and the black rabbit gives valuable contrast to the nearer one, a means of producing effect most useful in book illustration ; fig. 12, a dragon with bats' wings typical of the symbolic forms seen on illuminated manuscripts of the early Gothic period.

Plate XXIII.

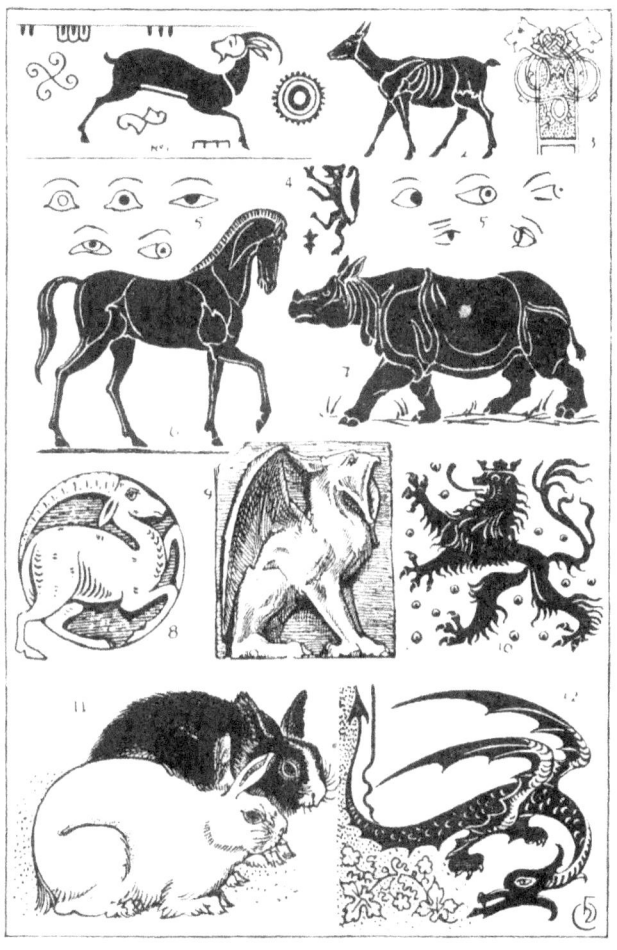

QUADRUPEDS AS ORNAMENT IN DIFFERENT MATERIALS.

Plate XXIV.

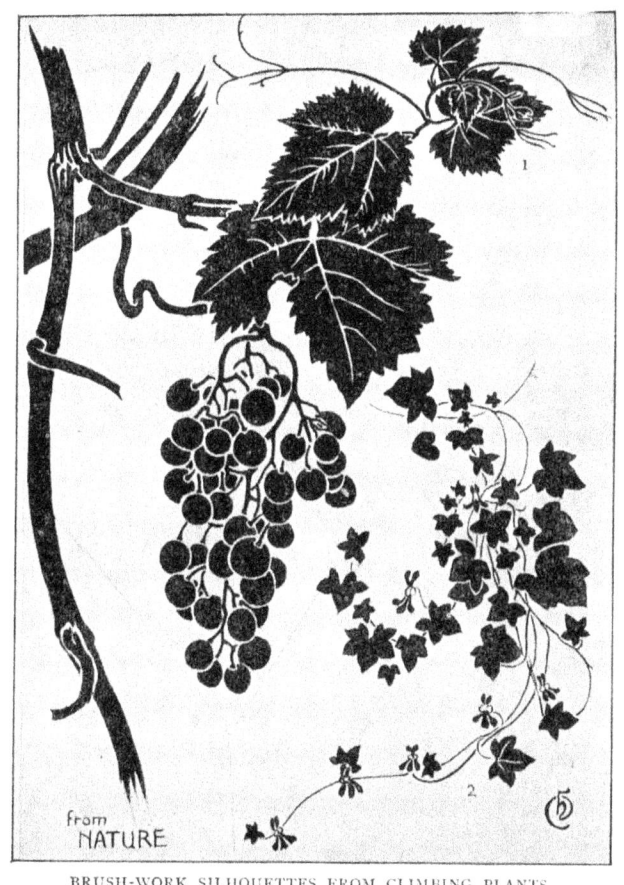

from
NATURE

BRUSH-WORK SILHOUETTES FROM CLIMBING PLANTS.

Plate XXV.

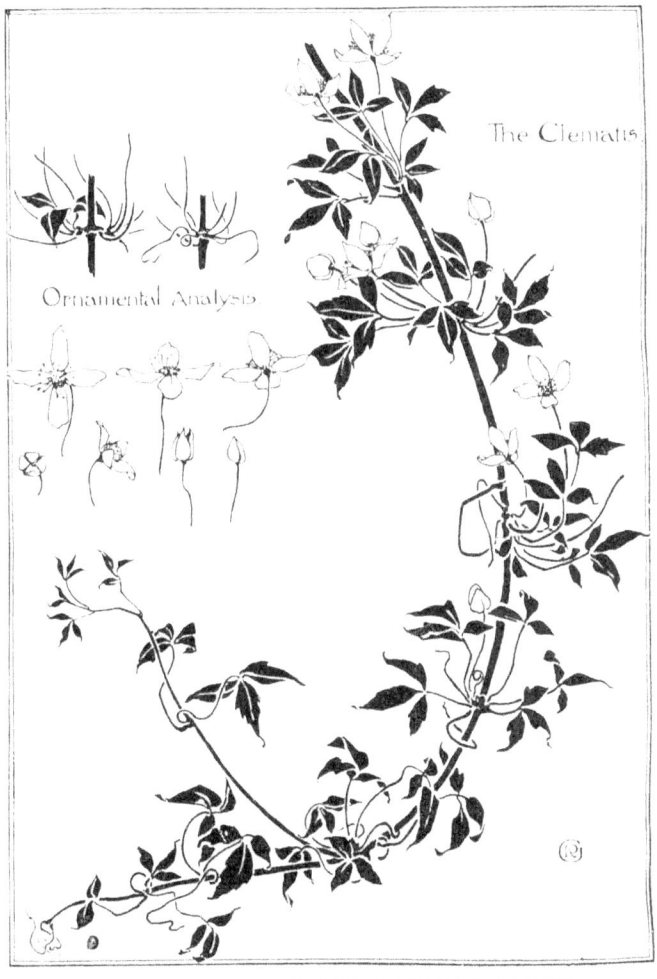

The Clematis.

Ornamental Analysis

BRUSH STUDY FROM NATURE BY RICHARD GLAZIER.

Plate XXVI.

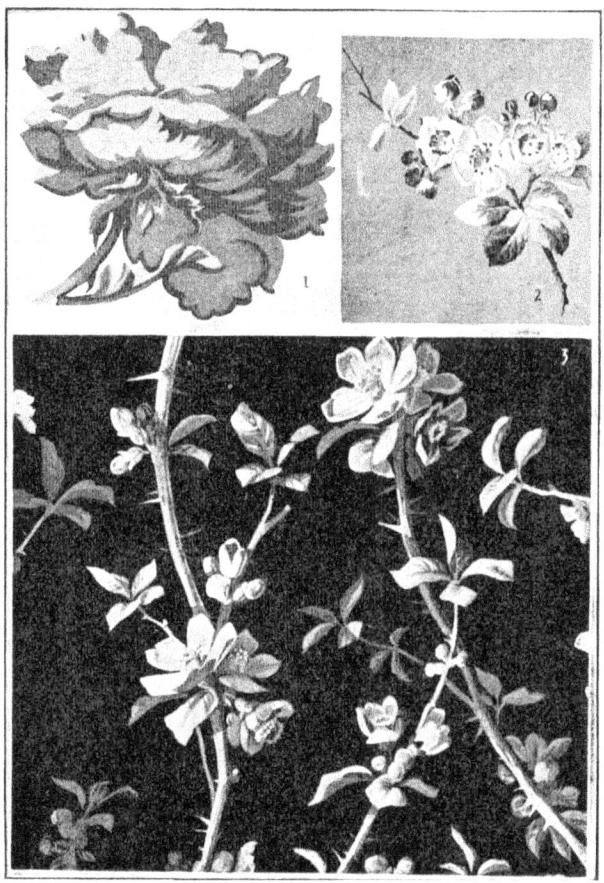

REALISTIC EFFECTS IN STEPPED TONES OF COLOUR. FRENCH.

PLANTS.

Plate XXIV. shows silhouette brush studies of plants taken direct from Nature, a treatment of great use to the decorator. The young grapes do not hide the stems, so that the construction is clearly seen. The lighter and freer character of fig. 2 is in pretty contrast, the leaves following each other in effective curves and sizes.

Plate XXV. is a brush rendering, of the clematis, and illustrates the lithe, active character of the "travellers' joy."

Plate XXVI. gives three examples of realistic treatments as generally used for cotton and wall-paper printing for certain markets. The tones are stepped definitely, so that an engraver could trace the area of each patch of colour. There is no softening of one tone into the other, and this kind of work is best for large decorations, in which distance will give sufficient blending. Softened work under such conditions would look weak and insipid. Fig. 3 is a good specimen of French tone work, in which it should be noticed that all the silhouette is lighter than the ground, and the highest lights are used sparingly.

CHAPTER VI.

INFLUENCES IN STYLE.

MONOCHROME ORNAMENT.

ON Plate XXVII. are two specimens of monochrome, of the kind usually given in the
government examination. The tones here are
crisp, and in fig. 1 three tones only are used.
Fig. 2 is a brush rendering of a Roman acanthus
scroll. Monochrome studies of still-life objects,
such as a dark bottle, and white jar and fruit
grouped together, give excellent practice in tone
work.

Plate XXVIII. shows portions of foliage from
illuminated manuscripts of the twelfth to the
fourteenth centuries, excellent examples of brush
work, rich in colouring and beautiful in effect. The
drawing for this plate was made on brown paper,
with zinc white and gum as directed, and lamp
black for the darkest tone, whilst the intermediate
tone is a mixture of both. This applies also to
Plates IX., XXII., and XXVI., but they were
worked on a laid ground on drawing paper.

Plate XXVII.

MONOCHROME PAINTING IN THREE TONES.

Plate XXVIII.

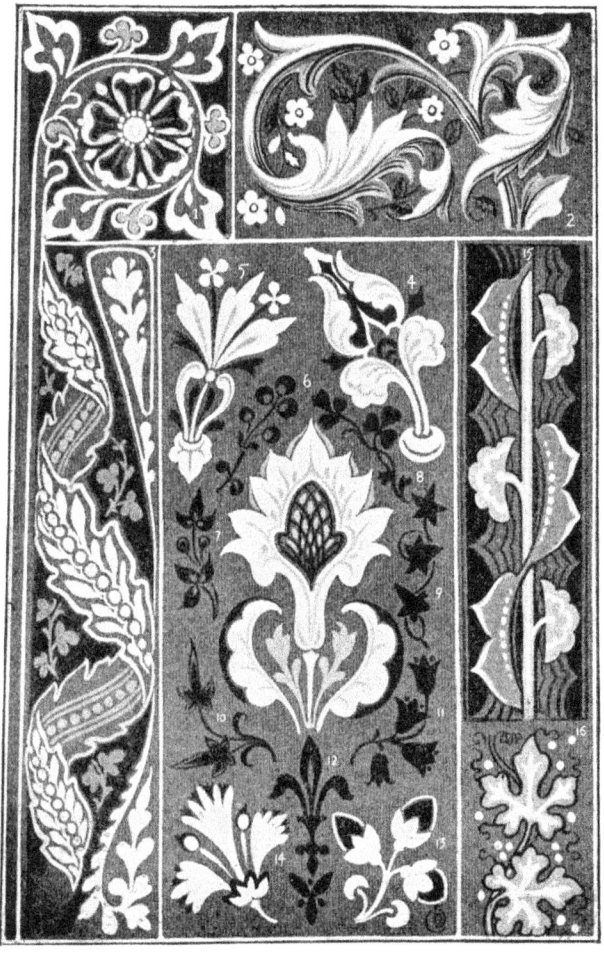

BRUSH-WORK DETAILS FROM GOTHIC MANUSCRIPTS.

Plate XXIX.

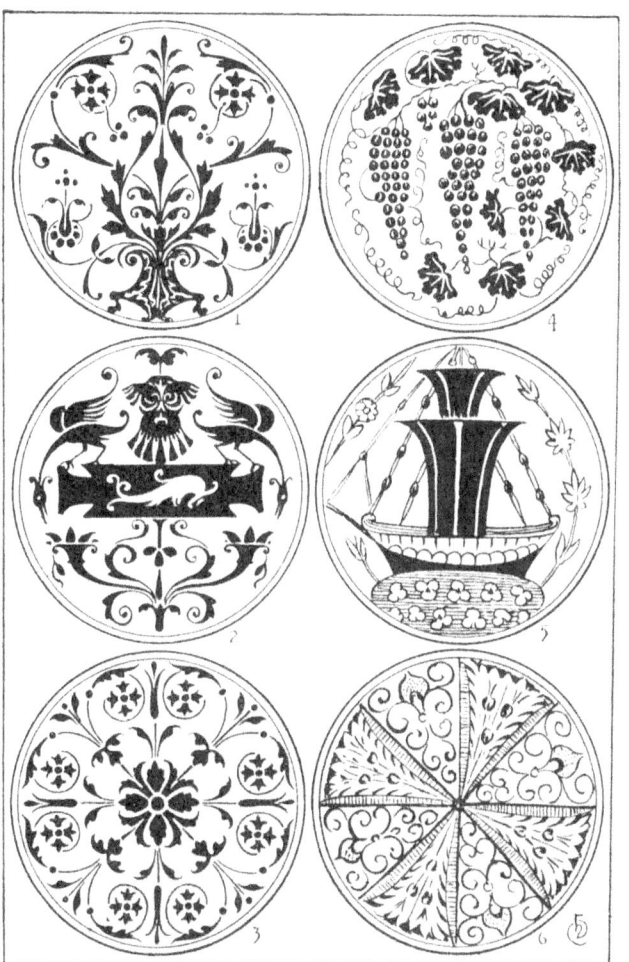

1, 2, 3, INLAID WOOD; ITALIAN.
4, 5, 6, PAINTED POTTERY; EASTERN.

SPACE FILLING.

Figs. 1, 2, 3, on Plate XXIX., are examples of space filling, taken from inlaid wood panels of the Italian Renaissance, showing the characteristic foliage and grotesque creatures used at that time. Figs. 4, 5, 6, are examples of Persian and Turkish pottery painting from the South Kensington Museum, showing very different motives and effects, essentially of brush work, and very beautiful with the rich floated colours.

Plate XXX. is from a German carved door of the fifteenth century, and as a lesson in space filling it is very valuable. The ornament is not alike on each side of the central figure, but is beautifully balanced. As an example of "saved" figure it is very good, and the sunk ground spaces are evenly distributed and economical in the matter of carving. Such a decoration will afford exercise in translation and adaptation for other purposes and with other details. The running borders and lock plate are full of suggestion for painted work.

LANDSCAPE.

On Plate XXXI. are bits of landscape in black and white silhouette, useful exercises in rendering the character of objects by carefully shaped masses. Evening and early morning present effects of this nature, but of course with much paler tones in the distance. Studies of this class of subject are effective in three tones, say the sky lightest, the mountains medium, and the foreground dark, or say, fig. 5, the moon lightest, the sky half-tone, perhaps brown paper, and the mountains dark.

ART INSTINCTS.

The faculty for creating or forming something is inherent in man. His peculiar unpreparedness for existence compels the making of shelter, clothing, etc., and of tools devised to assist him in his struggle, while the whole realm of Nature is laid under contribution in order to provide for his necessities. His inherent love of beauty also demands satisfaction, and a desire to reproduce Nature's charms causes the exercise of his imitative powers. By means of line, colour, or relief, render-ings of animals and plants, the decorations on natural objects, such as stripes, spots, and other markings, are used as ornament, or to represent interesting objects and incidents.

We have already noticed that truthful renderings of animal form, incised on the bone weapons of pre-historic times, give evidences of observation and skill of no mean order. A similar fondness for communicating ideas is seen, in the recent work of uncivilised peoples, such as the Indian hunter, the aborigines of Australia, and not less in the serious attempts of the child at school, who

Plate XXX.

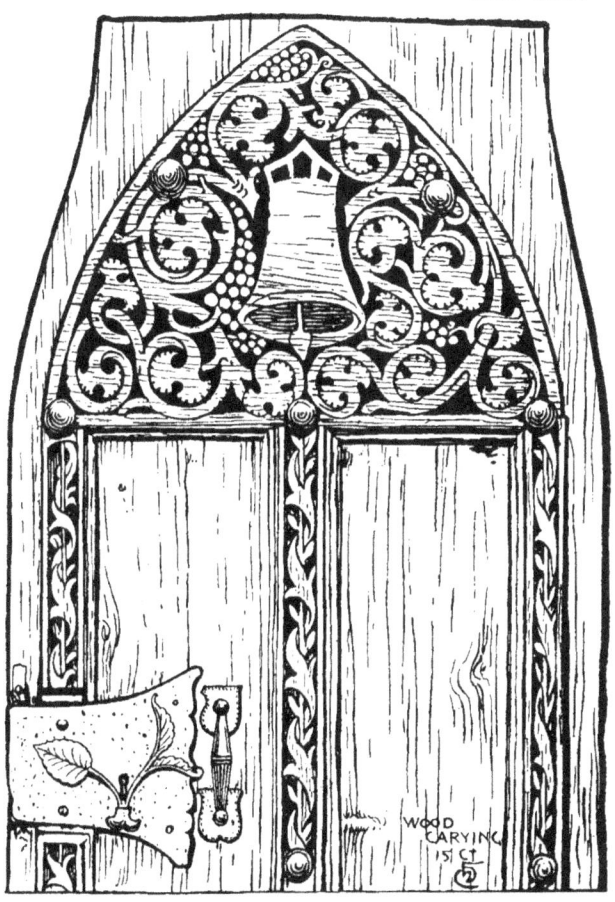

WOOD CARVING, "SAVED" PATTERN.

Plate XXXI.

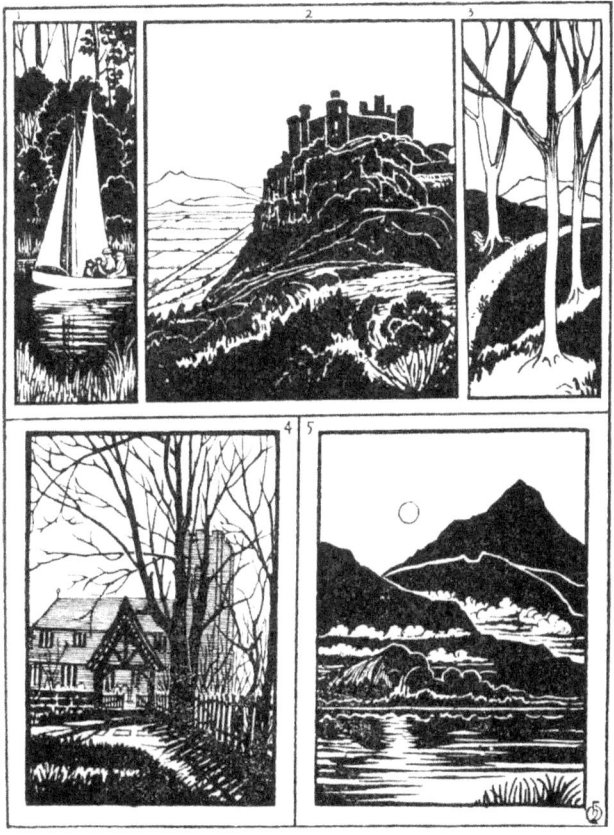

LANDSCAPES. LIGHT AND DARK SILHOUETTES DRAWN
WITH THE BRUSH.

endeavours to embody in a slate-pencil sketch the characteristics of an object, and though rude and wanting in grace and refinement of proportion, his sketch seldom fails in the intention.

An instinct seems to impel the tool-using animal to the employment of incising, marking, or surface-varying tools, on the materials readiest to his hand. The bone knife engraved with flint, the incised clay vessel or wooden paddle, the stained or tattooed skin, or the rough sculptured god of the Polynesian, give respectively types of the three principal aims : in the first, *representation* ; the second, *decoration* ; and the third, *symbolism*. Such classification has been aptly chosen by Owen Jones.

Picture-painting, or painting for the sake of realising and conveying a complete impression, and naturalistic sculpture, especially when coloured, provide many examples of the first class ; and in book illustration, relief sculpture, etc., according to the limitations of the materials employed, we have further examples.

The second class is shown in personal adornment and in beautifying the surroundings of home and public life. Textile fabrics, metal, glass, and pottery are ornamented with colour or relief, the natural beauty of the material being turned to good account, and the ornament being quite subservient to the object on which it is placed.

The third class gives us objects having distinct associations, which are intended to convey ideas.

These are not imitative of nature, but abstract or conventional, and often simplified to a mere diagram, in which the most characteristic features only are concentrated. Heraldry (Plate XXIII., fig. 10) gives us beautiful examples, and in the Egyptian, Byzantine, and mediæval Gothic styles symbolism is very frequent. It has been noted that letters serve to symbolise sounds, just as numerals express quantities.

Generally speaking, the art work of the past expresses the character, customs, and tastes of the period of its production. A style or phase is evolved gradually from some preceding it, and is effected by social and religious changes, and often by individuals of original ideas. Such influences act and re-act, and in the best periods a beautiful vitality is evident. Amongst many other factors which contribute to the formation of a style, that of commercial intercourse is one of the most remarkable.

The facilities of modern times, in railway, steamboat, and printing, have effected wonderful changes and have brought about the mixing of styles, each style possessing certain individual beauties whilst associated with the country of its origin, but often presenting a chaotic effect when unskilfully adapted to modern uses.

In olden times the changes of style were brought about gradually, often with very beautiful results, and they lasted for some considerable period. In

recent times changes are so rapid, that they uproot
and transplant before any proper development has
taken place, and much that is beautiful is lost ;
but at the same time we are perhaps spared the
continuance of much that is bad, and of many
incongruities.

Facilities for reproduction have tended to separate the craftsman and the designer—probably to
the advantage of the commercial side, but certainly
very often to the detriment of the artistic.

Thus, art reflects national life, and a deep study
of this branch of the subject demands some knowledge of national history. Books treating on the
historic styles and their peculiarities are numerous,
and different classifications are adopted in them,
some being arranged according to materials, others
by periods, and in the absence of the actual
objects, and even for museum study, they enable
comparisons to be made which will be most
valuable to the student.

DESIGNING.

The word " designing," in the constructive sense,
may be taken to mean the planning or creating
of something for a definite purpose, in which all
the parts employed produce a perfect and useful
whole, even apart from any special consideration
of its ornamentation, such as a house, a cabinet,
a vase, etc. In another sense, it may mean the

devising and disposing of beautiful forms for orna-
menting the useful object.

A designer might also be the craftsman, shaping
the clay, wood, or metal to express his own idea ;
but he is generally one who conceives the form of
the object and its decoration, and expresses or
marks them down by means of lines, colours, etc.,
on paper for the guidance of the craftsman ; all
calculated and set out to ensure a perfect final
result.   The architect acts in this capacity, as the
name (chief contriver) implies, and in his most
successful work there is neither paucity nor ex-
travagance in the use of the materials.

From such considerations we may gather that in
designing, the *use* of the object, the *position* it is to
occupy, and the *materials* of its composition, are
primary factors, which determine the proportion,
scale, and shape of it ; and if carefully considered
will generally result in an object of beauty.   For
instance, in a common water bottle the bulb is
lowest, for purposes of stability and gravity ; the
neck long, and closed to prevent evaporation and
the entry of dust ; the neck also serves as a handle
to grasp.   Being of crystal, the bottle displays the
sparkling water, a bubble, perhaps iridescent, reflecting surrounding objects ; and it is easily
cleansed—fused weed and sand from coast or
mountain side, associated in this form with rain-
drops pure from heaven, thus fulfil its purpose
beautifully.   Such is generally the case when a thing

Plate XXXII.

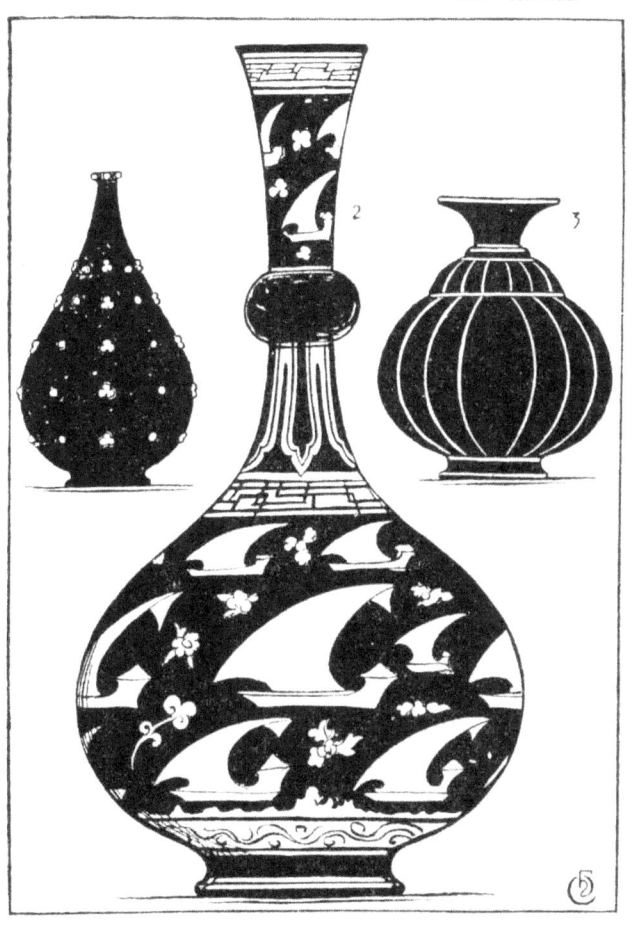

WATER BOTTLES, EASTERN, ILLUSTRATING PROPORTION.

is perfect, and probably the ugliness of many modern things is mainly because they are not yet perfected. The Persian water-bottles on Plate XXXII. are good examples of *fitness* for their purpose.

Design, then, implies the contriving of things for certain ends, artistically and economically, whether in the material itself or by means of diagrams and drawings. This should be kept clearly in mind, even in the most elementary stages of design, and all exercises should be associated with some definite purpose. In space filling, for instance, a square might be for a handkerchief, tile, or door panel; a circle for a plate, table-top, etc.; and the material should be stated always.

Nature is a sure guide in the perfect adaptation of means to an end. The common poppy head (Plate XXXIII.) may serve as an illustration of one of the numerous examples. The flower on its tall stem, soft and pendant in the bud state (fig. 2), becomes erect when the opening calyx (fig. 3) falls away, the rich-coloured papery petals expand and reveal a wealth of stamens surrounding a beautiful green seed vessel (fig. 4). After exposure to the sun, air, and insect life, the petals and stamens wither, leaving the seed-vessel with its fertilised seeds (fig. 5) standing alone on the now stiffened stem, enlarging and developing; the roof and overhanging eaves shelter closed valves. With the ripening warmth, the seeds are loosened from the cell walls, the valves burst open with the collapse of the roof, and the seeds are distributed by the action of the wind jerking the seed vessel on its stem, like pepper from its box.

This natural process illustrates perfectly the influence of the internal parts on the exterior; the cell walls causing facets (fig. 6), the filets (fig. 8) on which the sepals and stamens stood, the eaves (fig. 9), and cone roof (fig. 10) all indicating that good construction is beautiful and need not be hidden.

In Gothic architecture, the construction is usually visible ; a church in this style has been described as a " glorified barn," its rafters, beams, pillars, joints of masonry in the interior, serving as the basis for the distribution of decoration.

In the Greek style, the beam, column, and other structural parts are visible, and are refined and chastened in their proportions, the simple ornaments showing the most delightful appreciation of the beauty of wholeness.

A constant study of Nature's methods will afford the observer endless beautiful suggestions, and will fully exercise the selective and adaptive powers of the artist, to the benefit of his original work, while exciting his admiration.

One soon discovers that certain features are constant in the same species, that the character of the details affects the whole, every part being in perfect *harmony*, and in such *unity* as to give the most perfect lesson in designing.

Plate XXXIII.

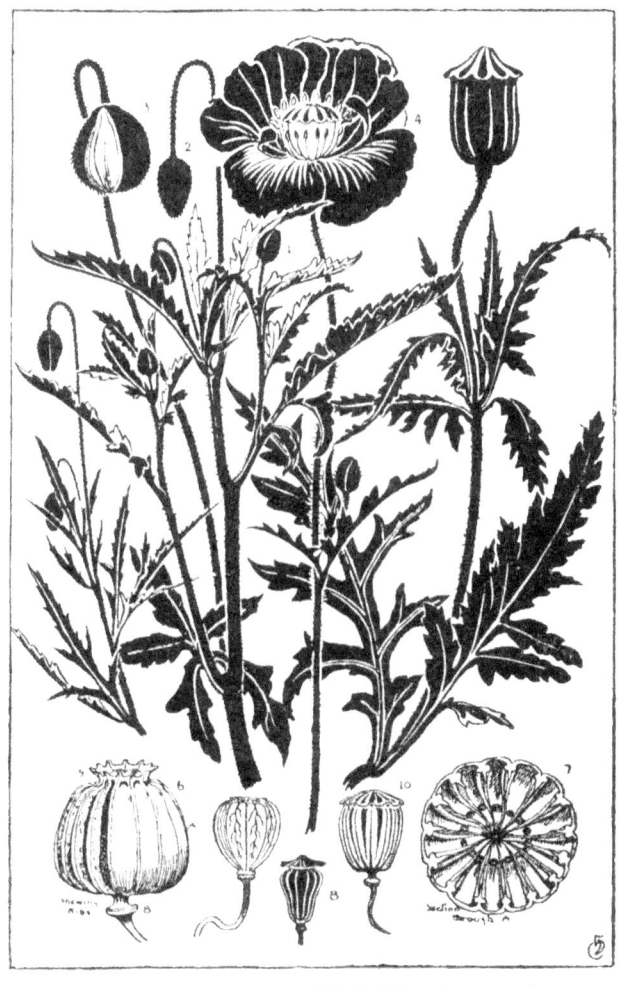

POPPY. BRUSH WORK, ILLUSTRATING "DESIGN."

A growing plant well illustrates this. The similarity of the rugged oak to its rugged leaf, of the rounded sycamore to its palmate leaf, the rhododendron with its discs of leaves, and spherical flowers, are examples; furthermore, a plant arranges itself in harmony with its surroundings.

A plant growing in the angle of a rock adapts itself so that the masses and lines are in graceful harmony and form a complete group, while another plant of the same kind growing in the open, adopts a more symmetrical arrangement. Wind-blown trees on the sea-coast are bowed permanently by prevailing winds; the forced growth of vegetables, the effects of pruning, and the recuperative power displayed in healthy nature, give striking illustrations of adaptation to circumstances, with a certain resultant beauty.

ORNAMENT.

We have already noticed that ornament of various periods, and in different materials, has certain predominating elements, which give it a distinct character. A change in construction, process, or in the customs of a people, alters the style, and, just as in Nature consistency of treatment is seen, so in the old art work of the best periods, details of a definite character are found in perfect harmony.

Ornament may be said to be that which is

added to adorn and make objects beautiful and interesting, without detracting from their use. It may also emphasise and explain certain characteristics, and render the object still more useful.

The decoration of Greek pottery gives good examples of delightful contours, beautified by simple abstract forms from Nature, so arranged subject to certain laws as to be in complete harmony with the object; units repeating in bands at regular distances, and connected with lines of growth; together with bands of figures, illustrative of ceremonies associated with the use of the vase. Thus, by simple painting in outline, or flat colour, the curved surface is preserved intact, and every line contributes to its beauty.

This is quite on natural principles—the rich colour-markings of the peacock and pheasant, the spottings upon butterflies' wings, and the markings on animals, such as the tiger, leopard, cat, etc.

It should be pointed out that much of this natural decoration is for protective as well as attractive purposes, some insects assuming the shape as well as the colouring of the leaves on which they feed.

In some styles of ornament certain types of foliage prevail, and give to it a distinct character; thus the lotus and papyrus of Egypt were used in both painted and sculptured forms, such as capitals of columns and in repeating patterns as symbolical of their rivers. Similar forms were adapted by the Assyrians, together with the palm tree; and in

Plate XXXIV.

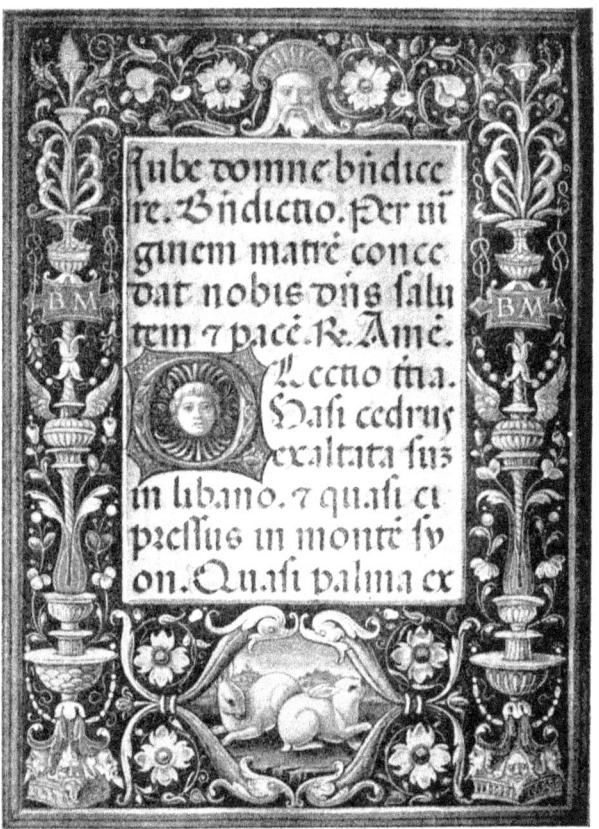

BRUSH AND PEN WORK.   ILLUMINATED MANUSCRIPT.
ITALIAN 15TH CENTURY, BRITISH MUSEUM.

the Greek style the same forms were used, but refined and beautifully varied, and more closely resembling the flowers of the honeysuckle. The vine, olive, and ivy were used direct from Nature, but reduced to the most simple silhouettes. Greek vase paintings show the use of such ornament for the decoration of costumes, as well as of pottery and the interiors of their dwellings.

In Roman ornament, the acanthus leaf (Plate XXVII., figs. 1 and 2) is most prominent, and was used for many centuries, while later in various modified forms it plays a great part in Renaissance work (Plate XXXIV). The ivy, vine, laurel, and olive, were also used; sculptured, or painted, and spaced pleasingly, but treated much more elaborately than the Greek foliage, and with greater variety of relief and picturesqueness, sometimes becoming confused and coarse. Ultimately, in the Byzantine style, these elements resumed a simpler decorative quality, and intertwined with other plants, which were symbolic of Christian ideas, finally formed the foundation of the early twelfth century Gothic foliage, used in sculpture, in manuscripts, and in stained glass, and suggesting the trefoil or clover leaf (Plates XXXV. and XXVIII.). In later Gothic, Nature was again reverted to, and fresh inspirations gave a peculiar charm of great value to its development.

This is beautifully illustrated in Longfellow's description of a monk in his scriptorium, who

holds up a book he is illuminating, and with pride
exclaims :

> There now is an initial letter,
> St. Ulric himself ne'er did a better,
> Finished down to the leaf and the snail,
> Down to the eye in the peacock's tail,

and so on, giving perhaps too real, too imitative
an effect ; for naturalism finally went to such an
extreme as to cease to be decorative.

During the period of this Gothic development
in Western Europe, the old Roman forms were
being revived in Italy, the ancient floral forms
were copied, and with true revivalist feeling fresh
inspirations from Nature—such as the lily, rose,
etc. (Plate XXXVI.)—were introduced. This
Renaissance spread over Europe, mingling with
the Gothic and ultimately supplanting it. So
that, from the twelfth to the sixteenth centuries,
the ornament in our cathedrals is seldom of the
acanthus type, adaptations of the trefoil and local
natural plants being chiefly used ; whilst in the
seventeenth and eighteenth centuries, the period
of the classic revival, the acanthus was of frequent
occurrence, and it was freely used until the Gothic
revival of fifty or sixty years ago.

It is instructive and interesting to notice the
commercial influences which bring about a change
of style. For instance, intercourse with the East
has given a steady flow of Oriental objects, such as
carpets, silks, and pottery, introducing details of an

Plate XXXV.

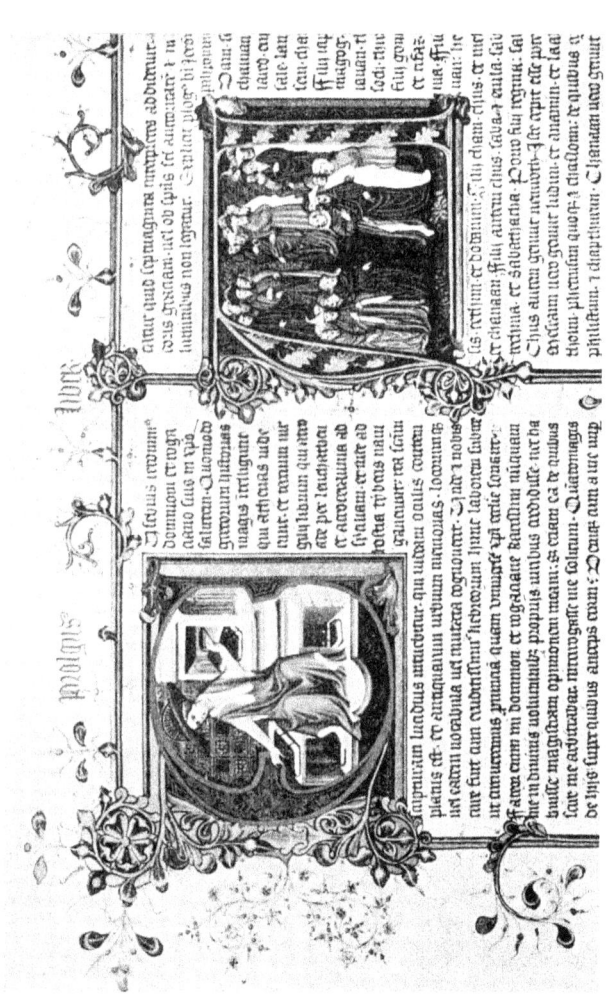

MANUSCRIPTS WITH MINIATURES. ENGLISH, A.D. 1400, BRITISH MUSEUM.

Plate XXXVI.

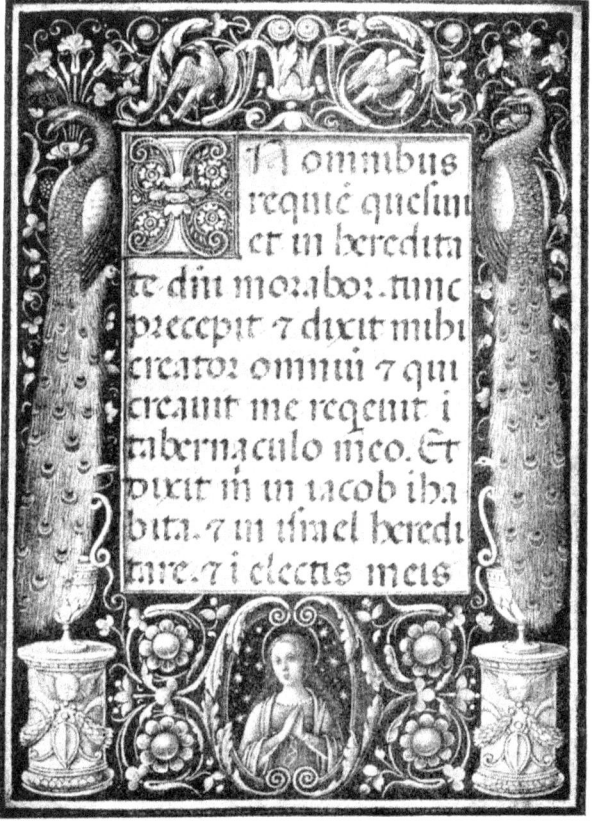

MANUSCRIPT IN GOLD AND COLOURS.
ITALIAN RENAISSANCE, A.D. 1480, BRITISH MUSEUM.

entirely different character from those used in the West, some, notably the Japanese, showing a close study of Nature, whilst others are of a nondescript kind, trammeled by religious laws and customs which prohibit the close imitation of natural forms.

In the Persian and Indian styles, renderings of the carnation, iris, hyacinth, and rose suggest a floral paradise; the carpets and tiles give such forms outlined and filled with the richest colours, and in the pottery the translucent effects of blue and green are very beautiful. We see the influence of this pottery in the Italian majolica, but combined with Renaissance foliage forms, and with an abundance of yellow and orange. Japanese and Chinese pottery are fully suggestive of brush working. The chrysanthemum, lotus, and peony are so treated as never to lose the character of the plant; the simple, direct painting shows a wonderful power of observation; the forms are generally rendered under influences which suggest activity and movement, as of the wind and storm bending the branches; moonlight mist, etc. Fans, lacquer, and textiles exhibit charming examples of dainty and tasteful decoration, which has been peculiarly influential in most recent styles.

In Venetian and Italian textiles of the fifteenth century the influence of Eastern fabrics is quite as marked as in the modern carpets, which also owe so much of their charm to Persian examples, and many nondescript forms now used might be traced, through a long period of devolution, back to some imported flower decoration.

Plate XXXVII. gives illustrations of woven fabrics. The square character peculiar to weaving is effective, and compensates somewhat for the absence of details. Figs. 1 and 2 are from fifteenth century German cloth-of-gold fabrics in the Manchester School of Art Museum ; fig. 3 is from an Egyptian tapestry in South Kensington Museum ; and fig. 4 from a Persian carpet—one half is squared, the other is left curved.

Plate XXXVII

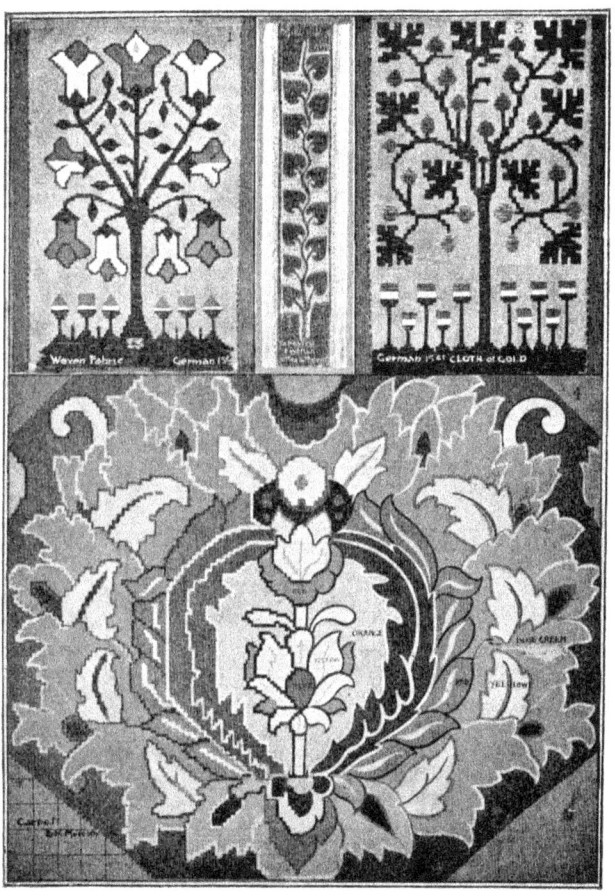

TAPESTRY AND CARPET, SHOWING WOVEN EFFECTS.

CHAPTER VII

APPLICATION OF STUDY

BRUSH STUDIES.

FACILITY and freedom are best gained by copying the same things many times, slowly at first, quickening as confidence is gained. The child should be taught to use a brush as early as the pen, and a systematic course should be followed. After a few exercises, such as those on Plate XI., natural objects may be used—a few tree stems and sprays of evergreen leaves attempted, in dark silhouette or light on dark, and such plants as the daisy, in black and white on toned paper, the pupil holding the plant in the left hand, and expressing something of the local tones, dark flower and light leaf, or light flower, dark centre, and dark leaf. Variegated leaves, shells, and butterflies will give most interesting practice, and such figures as those on Plates XX. to XXV. will form good exercises later. The importance of building up the parts and realising the proportions must ever be kept in mind. The

relative sizes of the parts and their direction or
pose must be correct. A goose walks with body
and neck at a different angle from that of a stork
or penguin ; the greyhound and reindeer, charger
and dray-horse, should be compared, and the
memory impressed with the movement of the
creatures. The Japanese draw a creature so often
as to be able to draw it from memory in any
position. For this purpose a bowl of goldfish or a
cage of birds will be useful. So the study of form
and action will be ensured.

Another series of studies might be directed to
decorative details. A bird's wing, for instance,
shows wonderful construction and decorative effects
of a most valuable kind for the cultivation of taste
for coloured ornament. Shells, fruits, flowers, etc.,
will show that each natural object has a distinct
scheme of colour, either warm, cool, low-toned, or
brilliant.

At an early stage colour work should be taken
up, beginning with the primaries—red, blue, and
yellow—using two, say blue and yellow, with
greens resulting from mixing in different proportions, then red and blue, red and yellow, and
their secondaries. Proceed from these to other
mixtures, using nature's schemes, and trying to
match them accurately, remembering that a little
carefully done will be the most instructive.

In colour harmony the feather of a peacock or
pheasant, or a pecten or nautilus shell, or even

a mussel shell, will afford good contrasting effects. Care should be taken to get the same tones as well as the tints, and the proportions or quantities, and their relative positions should be noted.

The most beautiful effects in nature are often the most transient. Ruskin gives a vivid description of a beautiful sky : " From the zenith to horizon becomes one molten, mantling sea of colour and fire ; every black bar turns into massy gold, every ripple and wave into unsullied, shadowless crimson, and purple and scarlet, and colours for which there are no words in language." Pigments fall far short of the reality ; nevertheless, make memory notes of these transient effects, as they will not only afford good training, but will be useful for rendering in design. For this purpose the following colours might be added to the three already mentioned—cobalt and French blue ; rose madder, brown madder, and burnt sienna ; cadmium, aureolin, and yellow ochre. For some of the most brilliant colours of flowers, pure scarlet, ruby madder, and cerulean blue are used, and in French designs brilliant colours derived from anilines are employed, but they are liable to fade and change colour.

MANUSCRIPTS.

Plate XXXIV. is from an Italian MS., and illustrates a characteristic treatment, in which delicate architectural details are used as the basis

for conventional plant form.   Masks, dolphins, and
wings are spaced evenly, and a simple pictorial
panel in the lower border gives interest and contrast.   Plate XXXVI. is from the same source,
and shows the use of acanthus scrolls surrounding
birds, and a cartouche, framing a saint, in the lower
part.   The symmetrical character of all the pages
in this MS. is very noticeable.

Plate XXXV. is from a MS., and is characteristic of the style of treatment prevalent in the
fifteenth century.   The initial letters are made the
chief feature, and balance of masses rather than
perfect symmetry is preferred.   The miniatures in
the letters are excellent examples of the simplified
form of figure painting, and show the same features
as those in glass painting and wall decoration of
the same period.

Plate X. is another example of an earlier MS.,
and the interest is centred in a decorative panel
effect with flat colouring.   Note the conventional
clouds, with symbols of the evangelists, and the
initial letters telling as effective spots of colour.
Outline and flat tints are used here, whilst
in Plates XXXIV. and XXXVI. monochrome-
toned effects are used.

Plate XXXVIII. gives examples of letters from
pottery of the seventeenth century in the British
Museum.   They are painted in slip on a dark
ground, and show the blot character peculiar to a
full brush stroke (figs. 1 and 2) ; fig. 5 is an alphabet

Plate XXXVIII.

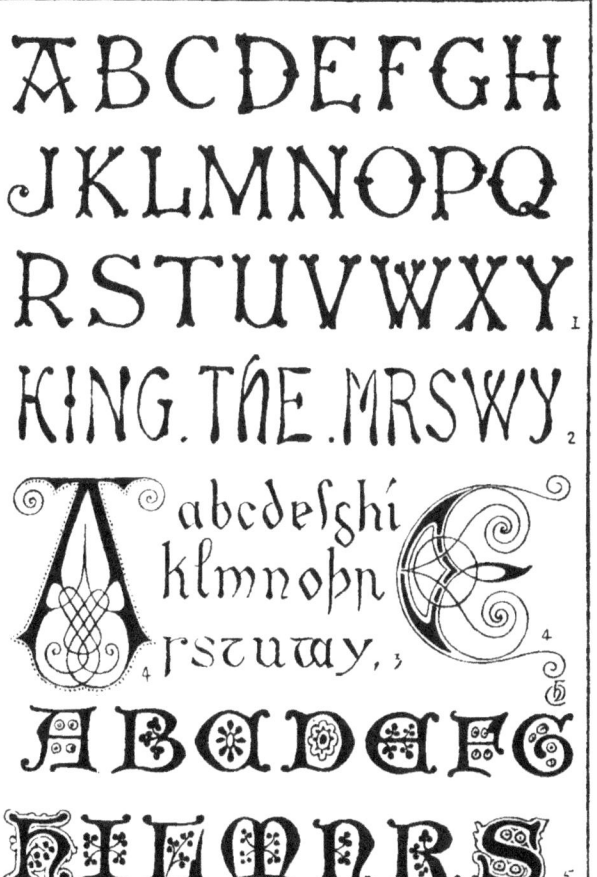

from a MS. of the sixteenth century, also in the British Museum—an ornamental, yet easily read type, suggestive of the brush. Figs. 3 and 4 are seventh-century letters, showing more the influence of the pen, the fine strokes and oblique angles being easily produced with that tool.

SUGGESTIONS FOR BRUSHWORK EXERCISES FOR ELEMENTARY AND SECONDARY SCHOOLS.

The following course is recommended for elementary classes in brushwork. It can be adapted to suit the age and capacity of the pupils, and for special purposes—for instance, as part of a general education, as manual training, or with an ultimate object of its application to designing. In any case, the aim should be, whilst giving an interest in the work, to cultivate observation and accuracy, without which facility is meaningless.

First to fourth exercises should be on white paper, with goose-quill sable, and black or brown stain, or deep blue water colour. Faintly indicate the distribution or position of the large masses with pencil. Paint the details of which these masses are composed directly with the brush.

Simple forms, such as Plate XI., figs. 1 to 4, 9 to 11, 18, 19, and 23 ; Plate XII., figs. 10 to 20, arranged on plans ; Plate XIV., figs. 13, 14, 21 to 23, 31 to 33 ; Plate XVII., figs. 10 to 12, 24 to 26. These might be adapted for the decoration of a book cover, table mat or painted fan, or some such object.

Fifth to eighth exercise on smooth brown or tinted paper, with white.

Compound forms : Plate XI., figs. 5, 6, 7, 14, 24 to 27 ; Plate XII., figs. 1 to 3 ; Plate XVII., figs. 5 to 9 ; Plate XIX., figs. 4, 10, and 11, 13 to 15, arranged on plans ; Plate XIII., figs. 6, 10, and 11 ; Plate XIV., figs. 7, 24 to 29 ; Plate XV., figs. 17 to 25 ; Plate XVII., figs. 10 to 15, 24 to 26.

These might be treated to serve as wall decorations, some as borders, others as fillings ; also for textiles, as the hem of a garment, a handkerchief, or of a banner ; of course, making them of such a scale as to be effective for their purpose.

Plate XXXIX. gives examples of treatments for border decoration, and for filling angular shapes with forms conventionalised in an extreme degree. In figs. 1 to 2, 6, 8 the honeysuckle, thistle, and clover can be traced, whilst in figs. 11 to 12 more naturalistic treatment of the vine and rose are used. It will be noticed that the details are made to fill the shapes evenly, and they are brought up to the boundary lines. Fig. 1. illustrates counterchange of tones ; the border pattern being light on a dark ground, the centre filling would be reversed. In Plate XL. there are suggestions for the decoration of panels, such as book covers ; the class exercise books might be treated

Plate XXXIX.

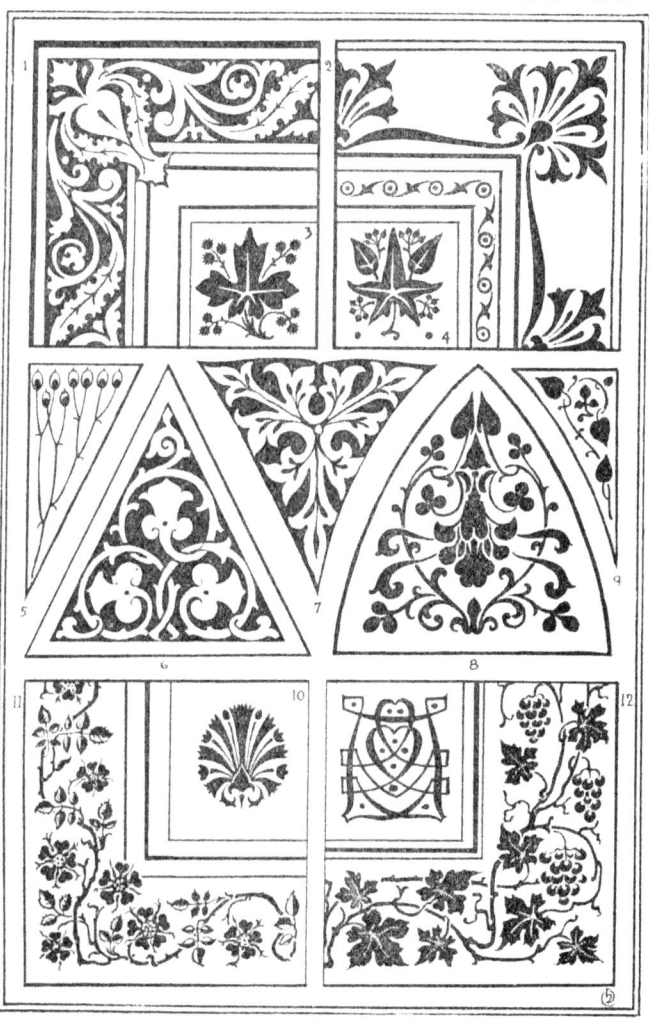

BORDERS AND FILLINGS OF ANGULAR SPACES.

Plate XL.

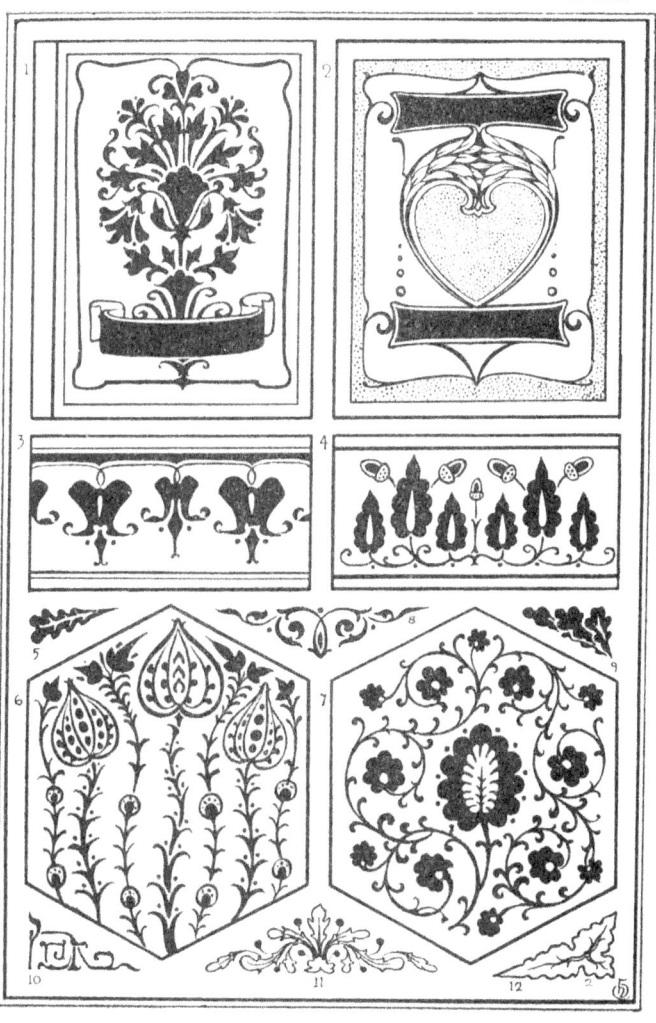

PANEL AND BAND FILLINGS.

Plate XLI.

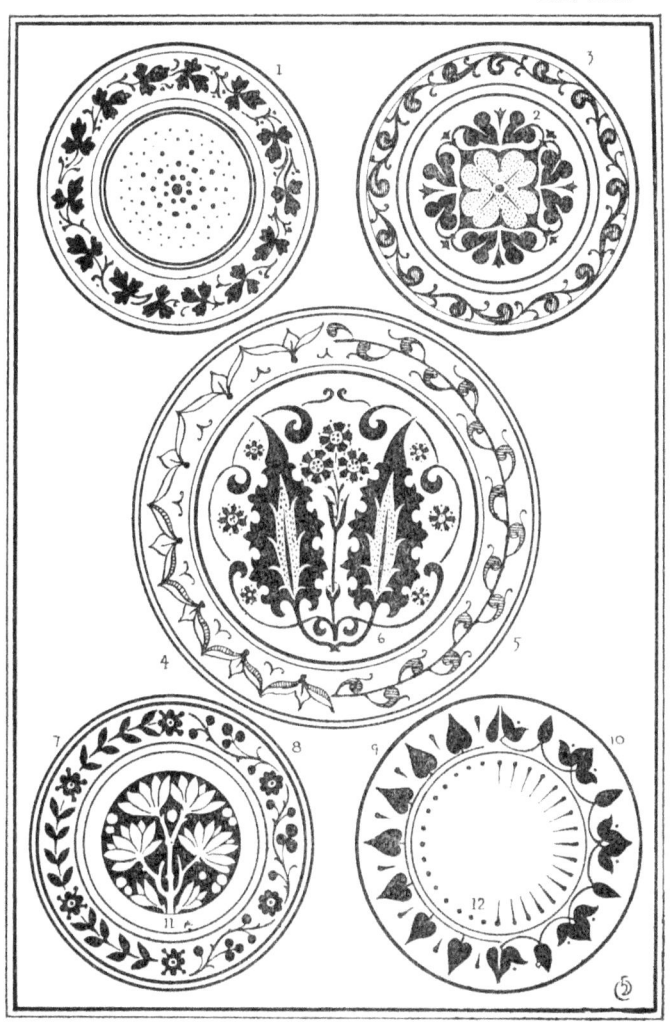

BORDERS AND FILLINGS OF CIRCLES.

simply in a similar way, the labels to bear the names of the pupil. Figs 6 and 7 are adapted from Eastern tiles; figs. 3, 4 show treatment of the lantern-flower and oak. These alternate arrangements are very effective in borders, and might be applied to curved bands and vases.

Such exercises, besides training the power of imitation, will give good practice in arranging and combining forms tastefully, and if accompanied by the painting of similar forms in tempera colour on small utensils, such as jam jars and bottles, they would compel consideration by associating the practice with its useful application (see Plate XIX., figs. 6, 12, and Plate XXXII.).

The fillings and borders of circles in Plate XLI. show details arranged on different plans; figs. 1, 3, 8, continuous or "running," the units of the repeats more or less emphasised with varied details. Figs. 4, 9, 10 are radiating borders which might be reversed to point inwards. The fillings are variously treated. Fig. 1, powdered; fig. 2, multi-symmetrical; fig. 6, bi-symmetrical; fig. 11, a balanced naturalistic growth: this circle also illustrates counterchange of tone. Experiments might be made in using other details on the same plans, and also in adapting the plans of these borders to straight bands.

Suggestions for working on rounded surfaces are given on Plate XLII. Such decorating will exercise the ingenuity and taste of the pupil in a pleasing way. A cardboard gas shade, an envelope box, a cup, plate, etc., might be decorated in tempera or water-colour. Even though not a permanent means, yet it would enable somewhat the realisation of effects produced on different surfaces, the scale and quantity of the ornament, and its arrangement in association with the object, all most important considerations in the application of ornament (see p. 2).

Lettering, as on Plate XXXVIII., gives units which demand careful spacing and shaping, and afford good exercise in making the ground and pattern of right relation to each other. The pupil's name inserted in a band of other ornament will prove attractive and helpful.

Ninth to twelfth exercises on light paper, with black, brown, or other dark colour.

Organic forms, such as Plate XIX., figs. 16 to 19, and Plate XXIII., figs. 1 and 2, should be copied. The proportions of body, head, neck, legs, etc., should be carefully observed. Plate XIX., figs. 20 to 24 show more elaborate treatments, the large divisions of the creatures being expressed with lines of the ground of equal thickness left to show how the masses are built up. Plate XXI., figs. 2, 3, 5, 8, 12, and 14 will exercise the pupil both in painting the figure and in "saving" it, by painting in the background, as in fig. 5 ; also in line and blot, as in figs. 2, 3, and 14, and Plate XXIII. figs. 6, 7, 10, 11, and 12. The two latter, like Plate

Plate XLII.

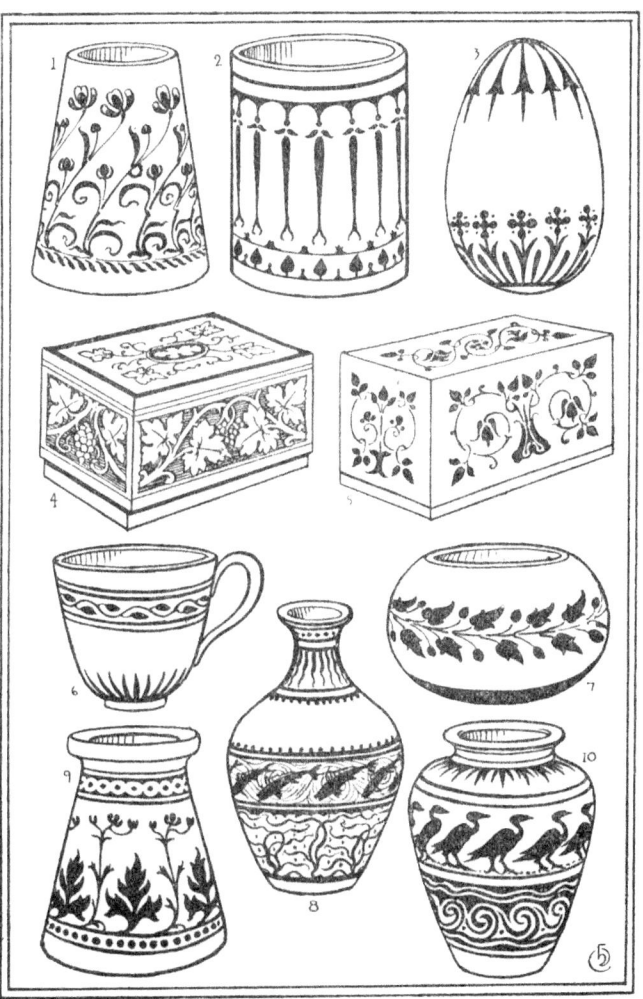

DECORATION OF SOLID FORMS.

XXI., fig. 12, are heraldic, and give the chief characteristics of the creatures strongly emphasised in a highly decorative manner.

These exercises should be extended at least to two lessons each, so that they can be thoroughly grasped. Variations will suggest themselves, and all should lead ultimately to working from natural objects. For this purpose common objects can be easily obtained, such as the poppy head, cockle, and pecten shell, insects and birds, while in foliage, evergreens, such as holly, laurel, and ivy, will be best for early study, as they are least likely to droop. All these might be treated as tone studies, using black and white and two brushes on tinted paper, similar to Plate XXIII. and Plate XXVIII., the original drawings of which were worked on brown paper in tempera colour. An alternative to the tone studies might be provided by using three primary colours, carefully matching from Nature. Such work is very fascinating, but unless done studiously it is disappointing and of slight use.

By means of the silhouette and tone studies the pupil will be enabled better to devote attention thoroughly to colour work, so as to render the quantities and tones effectively.

THE END.

INDEX

181